Introduction

This book supports students preparing for the AQA GCSE exam. The pract_
the book are carefully modelled after past papers and specifications of exam board to ensure that the papers as a whole provide a rich and varied practice to meet all requirements of GCSE mathematics with an appropriate difficulty.

Papers are designed to teach students the most easily applicable, reusable and fastest solutions to typical problems, and utilise problems which target areas of maths which students typically forget under the pressure of an exam. Solutions provided have been reviewed by many students to ensure that they are easily understandable while being the fastest and most re-applicable.

The practice papers cover the following six distinct topic areas:
1. Fundamental Number Operations
2. Algebra
3. Ratio, proportion, and rates of change
4. Geometry and measures
5. Probability
6. Statistics

After completing these practice papers, you should be able to:
1. Quickly formulate optimal solutions to any GCSE mathematics question.
2. More readily apply previously learnt skills on a question to question basis.

GCSE Mathematics Practice Papers comprises of 2 books, calculator and non-calculator. Each book contains 4 full practice papers, while each practice paper contains 25 questions and solutions.

Contents

1	Paper 1	1
2	Paper 2	14
3	Paper 3	27
4	Paper 4	40
5	Paper 1 solutions	54
6	Paper 2 solutions	66
7	Paper 3 solutions	77
8	Paper 4 solutions	87

Paper 1 (Non-Calculator)

Materials

For this paper you must have:
- mathematical instruments

You **must** not use a calculator

Time allowed

1 hour 30 minutes.

Instructions
- Use black ink or black ball-point pen. Draw diagrams in pencil.
- Answer all questions.
- You must answer the questions in the space provided. Do not write outside the box around each page or on blank pages.
- Do all rough work in this book. Cross through any work that you do not want to be marked.
- In all calculations, show clearly how you work out your answer.

Information
- The marks for questions are shown in brackets.
- The maximum mark is 80.

Advice
- Read each question carefully before you start to answer it.
- Keep an eye on the time.
- Try to answer every question.
- Check your answers if you have time at the end.

1   Circle the area that is the same as 20 cm²

    0.2 mm²   2 mm²   200 mm²   2000 mm²

    ....
    ....
                                                                    (2 marks)

2   Which of these represents the shaded region?
    Circle your answer.

    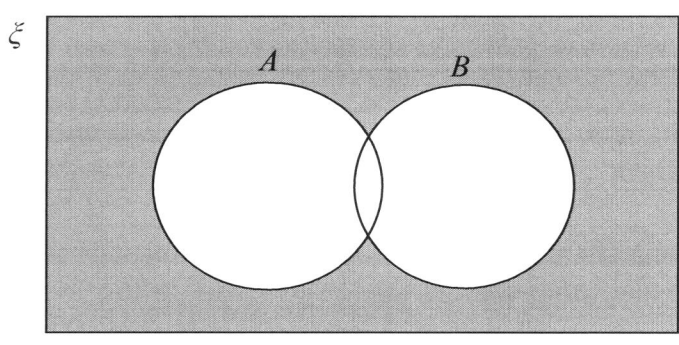

    $(A \cup B)'$ A' $(A \cap B)'$ B'

    ....
    ....
    ....
                                                                    (2 marks)

3   Emma invests £5000 for 5 years. The investment gets compound interest of 5% per annum.

    Which of these calculates how much the investment is worth at the end of 5 years?
    Circle your answer.

    $5000 \times (1+5\%)^5$ $5000 \times (5\%)^5$ $5000 \times (1+5 \times 5\%)$ $5000 \times (5 \times 5\%)$

    ....
    ....
    ....
                                                                    (2 marks)

4   Write $0.1\dot{3}\dot{6}$ as a fraction in its simplest form.

   Answer…………………………….   (3 marks)

5   The first four terms of an arithmetic sequence are

   7   13   19   25

   Work out an expression, in terms of *n*, for the *n*th term.

   Answer…………………………….   (3 marks)

6   Expand and simplify $(2+\sqrt{3})(3-\sqrt{3})$

   Give your answer in the form $a+b\sqrt{3}$, where *a* and *b* are integers.

   Show your working clearly.

   Answer…………………………….   (2 marks)

7   Factorise fully $4x^2 - 25$

   Answer…………………………….   (2 marks)

10

8   Simplify the expression $(3x^2y^3)^3$

    Answer……………………………. (2 marks)

9   Solve the equation $x^2 - 2x - 2 = 0$

    Give your answer in the form $a \pm \sqrt{b}$, where a and b are integers.

    Answer……………………………. (2 marks)

10 $a - 2b < 12$ and $a + b = 6$

    Work out the range of possible values of b.

    Give your answer as an inequality.

    Answer……………………………. (3 marks)

11 50% of p = 20% of q.

    Work out p as a percentage of q.

    Answer……………………………. (2 marks)

12   Without using a calculator, evaluate $\dfrac{\sqrt{32}+\sqrt{50}}{\sqrt{18}}$

Show all your working.

....

....

....

....

       Answer…………………………….   (2 marks)

13   Find an approximate value for $\dfrac{\sqrt{9.115}\times 10^{5}}{5.997\times 10^{-4}}$

Give your answer in standard form.

....

....

....

....

       Answer…………………………….   (2 marks)

14   Work out $2\dfrac{2}{3}\times 1\dfrac{5}{7}$.

Give your answer as a mixed number in its simplest form.

....

....

....

....

       Answer…………………………….   (2 marks)

15 Write as a single power of x

$$\left(\frac{x^{\frac{1}{3}} \times x^{\frac{5}{3}}}{x}\right)^2$$

....
....
....
....

Answer…………………………….   (2 marks)

16 Simplify $\dfrac{\sin 60° + \tan 30°}{\sin 45°}$

Give your answer in the form $\dfrac{a}{b}\sqrt{c}$, where a, b and c are integers

....
....
....
....

Answer…………………………….   (3 marks)

17 a, b, c and d are consecutive integers.

Prove that $ab + cd$ is always even.

....
....
....
....
....
....

(3 marks)

18 The square ABCD is drawn inside the regular octagon ABEFGHIJ. They share side AB.

Work out the value of x.

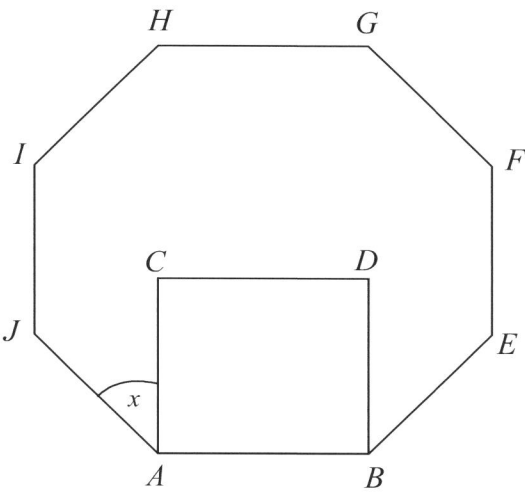

Answer……………………………. (4 marks)

19 ABCD is a quadrilateral.

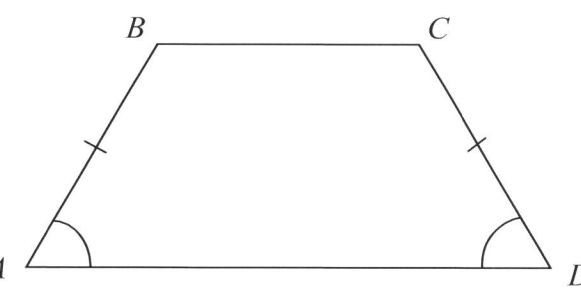

AB = CD.

∠BAD = ∠ADC.

Prove that triangle ABD is congruent to triangle DAC.

(4 marks)

20 The equation of the circle is $x^2 - 10x + y^2 - 4y + 13 = 0$.

20(a) Work out the coordinates of the centre of the circle.

....
....
....

Answer……………………………….   (3 marks)

20(b) Work out the diameter of the circle.

....
....
....

Answer……………………………….   (3 marks)

21   $P(2,4)$ is a point on a circle, centre O.

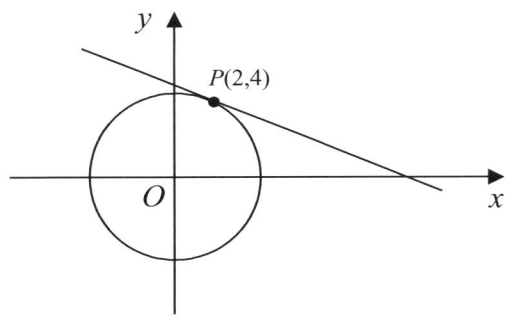

21(a) Work out the equation of the circle.

....
....
....
....
....
....

Answer……………………………….   (3 marks)

21(b) Work out the equation of the tangent to the circle at *P*.

Give your answer in the form $y = mx + c$

....

....

....

....

....

Answer……………………………. (3 marks)

22 $f(x)$ is a quadratic function.

The diagram shows part of the graph of $y = f(x)$.

Points $A(-1,0)$, $B(0,-2)$ and $C(4,0)$ lie on $y = f(x)$.

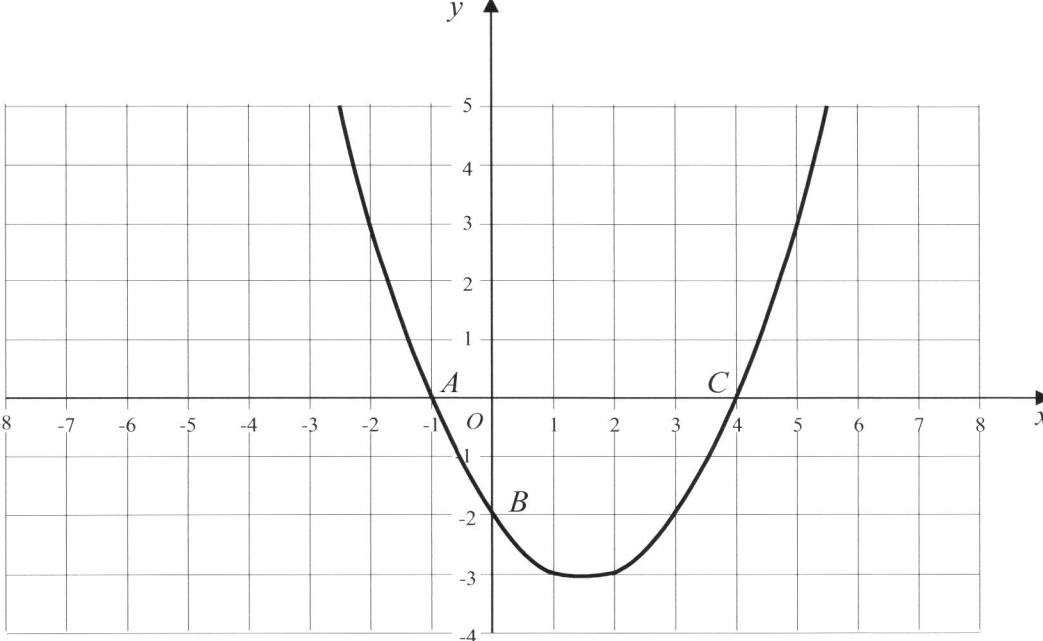

22(a) The graph of $y = f(x+4)$ represents a transformation of the graph of $y = f(x)$.

On the grid below, sketch the graph of $y = f(x+4)$.

On your graph mark clearly with crosses the images of A, B and C in the transformation. (4 marks)

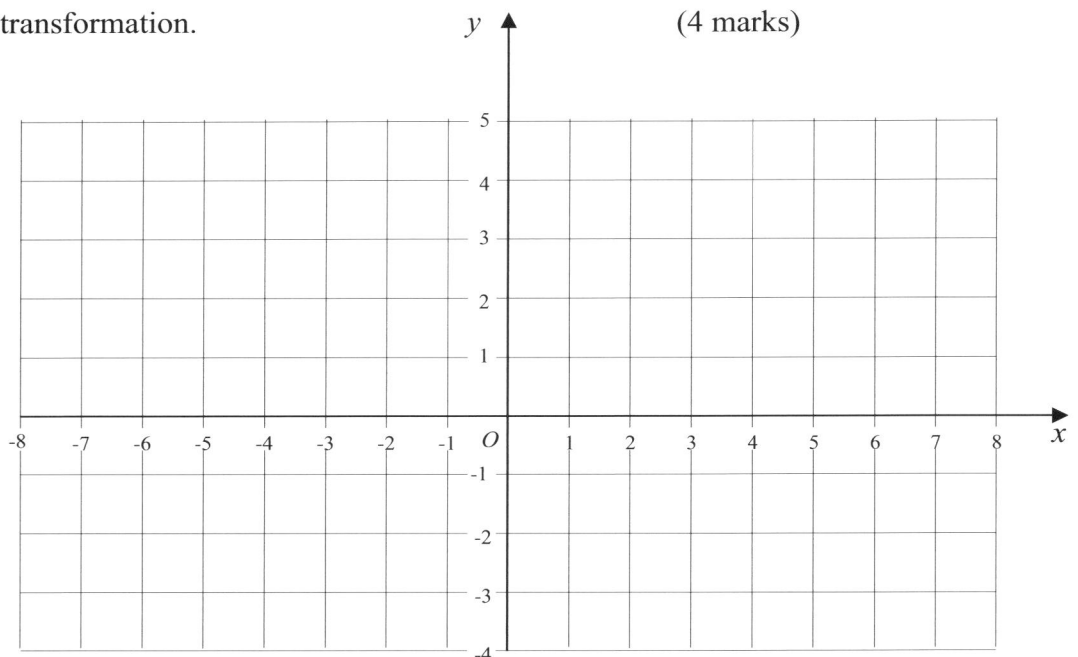

22(b) The graph of $y = f(-x)$ represents another transformation of the graph of $y = f(x)$.

On the grid below, sketch of $y = f(-x)$.

On your graph mark clearly with crosses the images of A, B and C in the transformation. (4 marks)

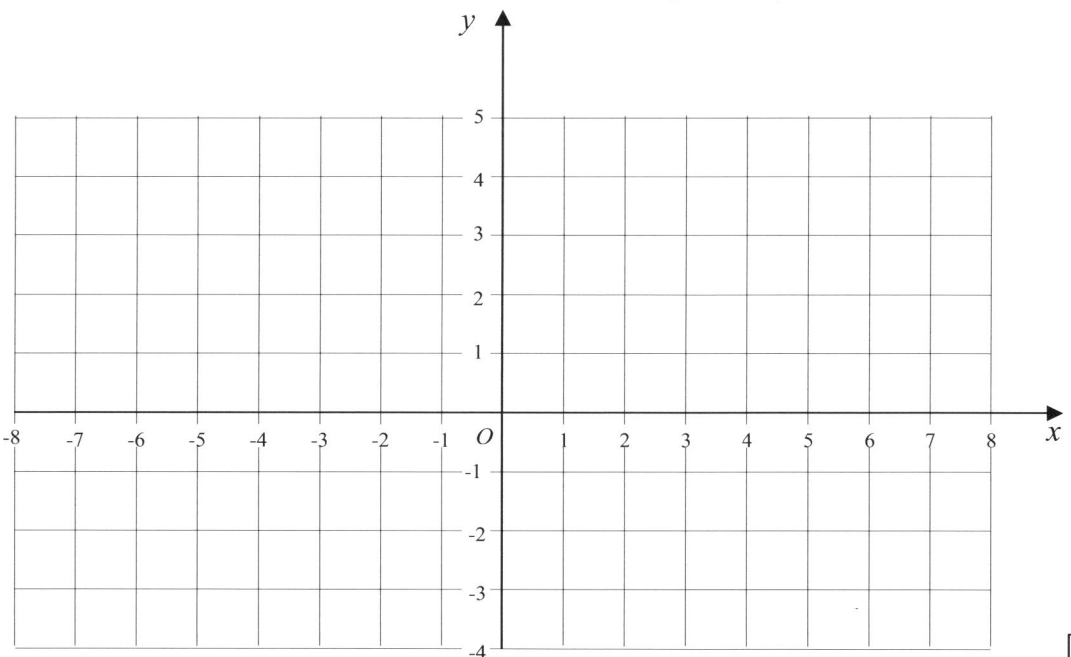

23 The four candidates in an election were A, B, C and D.

The pie chart shows the proportion of votes for each candidate.

Work out the probability that a person who voted, chosen at random, voted for A.

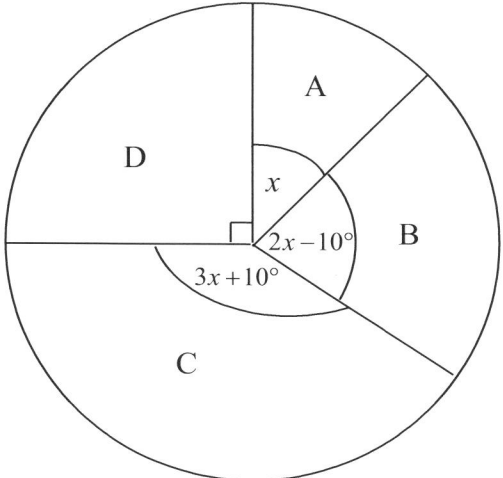

....

....

....

....

....

Answer................................ (4 marks)

24 The histogram gives information about the heights of 540 Christmas trees.

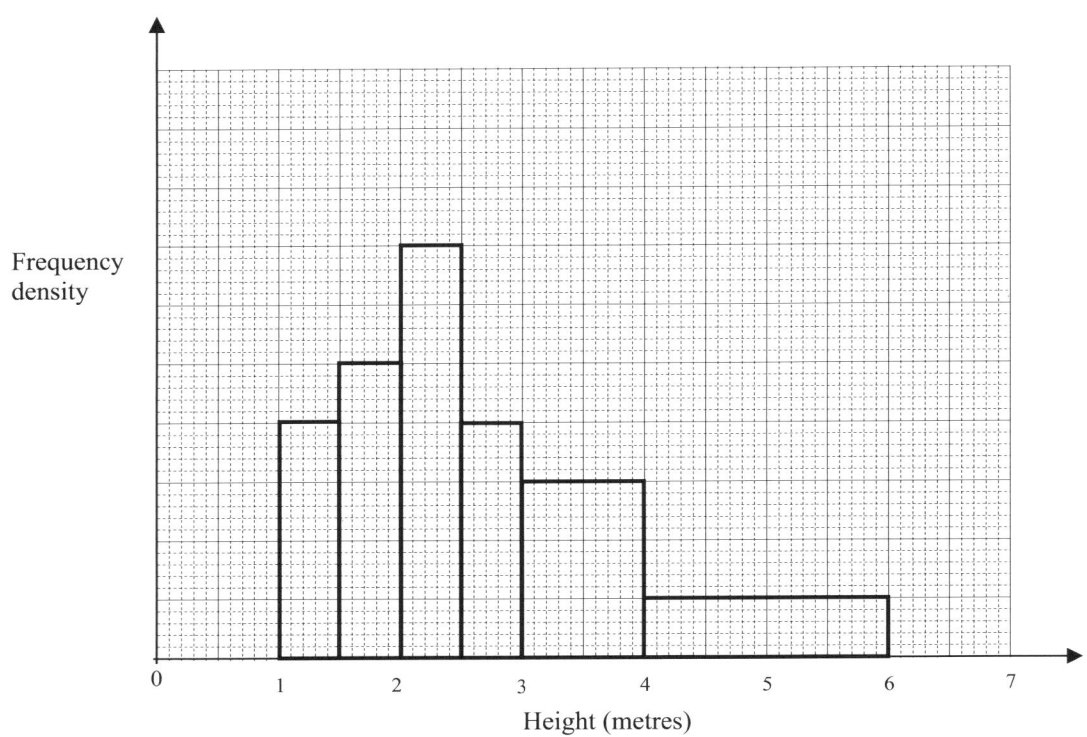

There is no Christmas tree shorter than 1 metre.

There is no Christmas tree taller than 6 metres.

Work out an estimate for the number of Christmas trees with a height greater than 3 metres.

....

....

....

....

....

....

Answer……………………………   (4 marks)

25   OABC is a parallelogram.

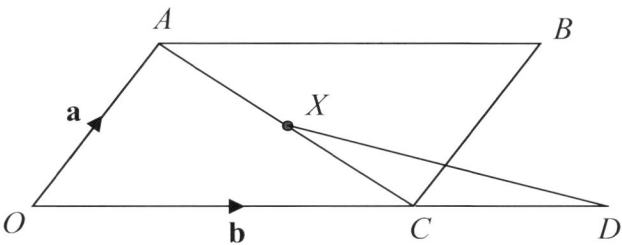

$\vec{OA} = \mathbf{a}$, $\vec{OC} = \mathbf{b}$

X is the midpoint of the line AC.

OCD is a straight line so that OC:CD = 2:1

Work out the vector of $\vec{XD}$

Give your answer in terms of **a** and **b**.

....
....
....
....
....
....
....

     Answer.................................   (5 marks)

Paper 2 (Non-Calculator)

Materials
For this paper you must have:
- mathematical instruments

You **must** not use a calculator

Time allowed
1 hour 30 minutes.

Instructions
- Use black ink or black ball-point pen. Draw diagrams in pencil.
- Answer all questions.
- You must answer the questions in the space provided. Do not write outside the box around each page or on blank pages.
- Do all rough work in this book. Cross through any work that you do not want to be marked.
- In all calculations, show clearly how you work out your answer.

Information
- The marks for questions are shown in brackets.
- The maximum mark is 80.

Advice
- Read each question carefully before you start to answer it.
- Keep an eye on the time.
- Try to answer every question.
- Check your answers if you have time at the end.

1 Simplify $(2^2 \times 2^3)^2$

   Circle the answer.

   2^{10} 2^{12} 4^{10} 4^{12}

   ....
   ....
   ....

   (2 marks)

2 On 1 April 2019, the cost of 5 grams of gold was £220. The cost of gold increased by 10% from 1 April 2018 to 1 April 2019.

   Circle the calculation for the cost of 5 grams of gold on 1 April 2018.

   $\dfrac{220}{1.10}$ 220×1.10 $220 \times (1 - 0.1)$ $\dfrac{220}{1.01}$

   ....
   ....
   ....

   (2 marks)

3 Circle the volume that is the same as 2.2 m³

   2.2×10^3 cm³ 2.2×10^6 cm³ 2.2×10^9 cm³ 2.2×10^{12} cm³

   ....
   ....
   ....

   (2 marks)

4   $x:y = 3:4$ and z is 20% of y.

Work out $x:y:z$

Give your answer in its simplest form.

....

....

....

    Answer……………………….   (2 marks)

5   Below are four equations:

Equation 1: $y = 3x - 3$;   Equation 2: $y = 2x^2 + 3$

Equation 3: $3x + 6y = 12$;   Equation 4: $y = 3x^3$

5(a) Match one the equations to each of the three graphs below:

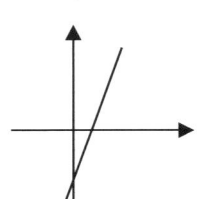

Graph A

Equation ……

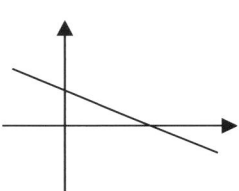

Graph B

Equation ……

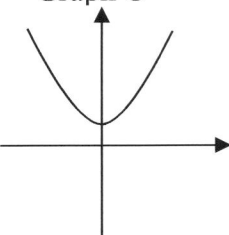

Graph C

Equation ……

(3 marks)

5(b) Draw the graph of the remaining equation on the axes below.

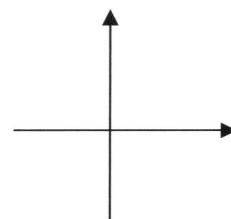

Equation ……

(2 marks)

6   Write $0.\dot{6}\dot{3}$ as a fraction in its simplest form.

   ....
   ....
   ....
   ....
   ....
   ....

               Answer................................   (3 marks)

7   A linear sequence starts
       3   10   17   24   …

   Work out an expression for the nth term.

   ....
   ....
   ....
   ....
   ....
   ....
   ....

               Answer................................   (3 marks)

8   Rationalise the denominator and simply fully $\dfrac{6}{3-\sqrt{3}}$

   ....
   ....
   ....
   ....

               Answer................................   (2 marks)

8

17

9   Solve the simultaneous equations

$2x + y = 15$

$x + y = 8$

....

Answer................................ (2 marks)

10 Solve $x^2 + 3x - 10 < 0$

....

Answer................................ (2 marks)

11 Express 72 as the products of its prime factors.

Give your answer in index form.

....

Answer................................ (2 marks)

12 The scale of a map is such that 2 cm on the map represents an actual distance of 10 km.

12(a) Express the scale of the map as a ratio in the form 1: *n* where *n* is an integer.

....

....

....

....

Answer……………………………. (2 marks)

12(b) The actual area of a park is 250 km^2. Calculate the area, in cm^2, of the park on the map.

....

....

....

....

Answer……………………………. (2 marks)

13 20% of a number is 150.

Work out the number.

....

....

....

Answer……………………………. (2 marks)

14 In a sale, all normal prices are reduced by 25%.

The normal price of a kettle is reduced by £3.00.

Work out the normal price of the kettle.

....

....

....

Answer……………………………. (2 marks)

15 Write 1.5×10^{-4} as an ordinary number.

....

....

....

Answer……………………………. (2 marks)

16 Work out the value of $2.2 \times 10^5 \times (4 \times 10^3)$

Give your answer in standard form.

....

....

....

Answer……………………………. (2 marks)

17 A large rectangle is made by joining four identical small rectangles as shown.

Diagram **NOT** accurately drawn

The perimeter of one small rectangle is 24 cm.

Work out the perimeter of the large rectangle.

....

....

....

....

....

....

....

Answer……………………………. (3 marks)

18 Triangle ABC has perimeter 16cm

$AB = 5$ cm.

$BC = 4$ cm.

Show that ABC is an obtuse triangle.

....

....

....

....

....

....

(4 marks)

19 Here are a trapezium and a right-angled triangle. The area of the triangle is the same as the area of the trapezium.

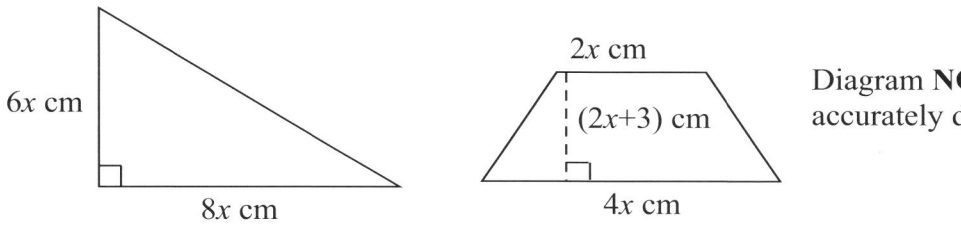

6x cm
8x cm
2x cm
(2x+3) cm
4x cm
Diagram NOT accurately drawn

Work out the value of x.

....

....

....

....

....

Answer................................. (4 marks)

8

20 *AB* is a diameter of this circle and is extended to point *S*. *ST* is a tangent meeting the circle at point *T*. *O* is the centre of the circle. *AT=AO*

Prove that triangle *ATB* is congruent to triangle *OTS*.

(4 marks)

21 Here is the graph of $y = f(x)$

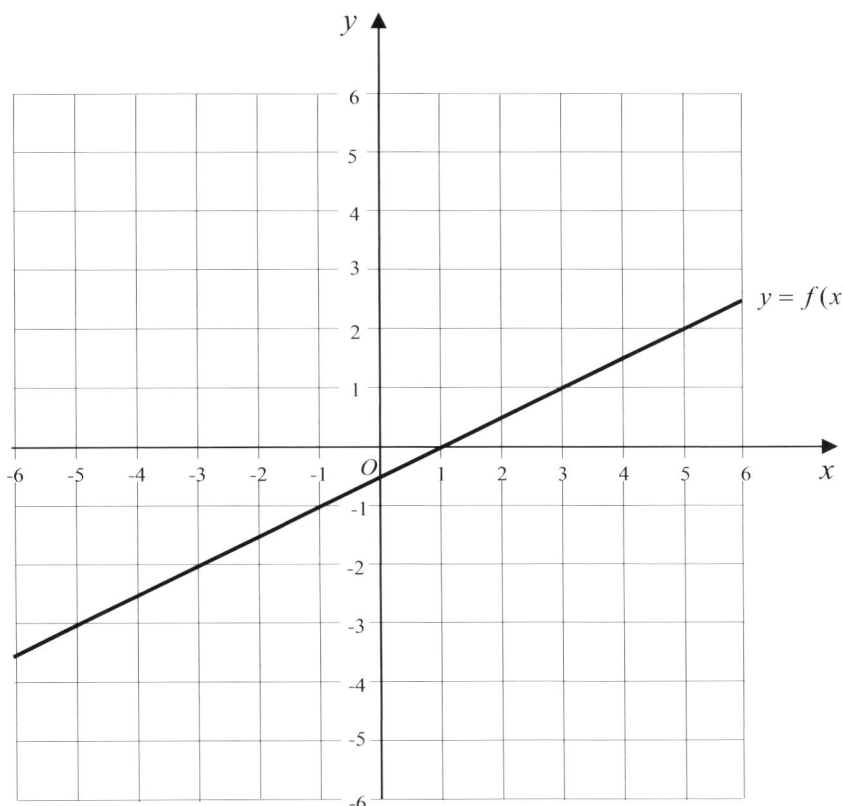

21(a) On the grid, draw the graph of $y = 2f(x)$

....
....
....
....
....

(3 marks)

21(b) On the grid, draw the graph of $y = 2f(x+2)$

....
....
....
....

(3 marks)

22 The diagram shows a solid prism with the same cross-section through its length. The cross-section is a right-angled triangle with height 30 cm. The base *ABCD* is rectangle of width 20 cm and length 40 cm. The prism is made from wood with density 0.0005 kg/cm³.

Work out the mass of the prism.

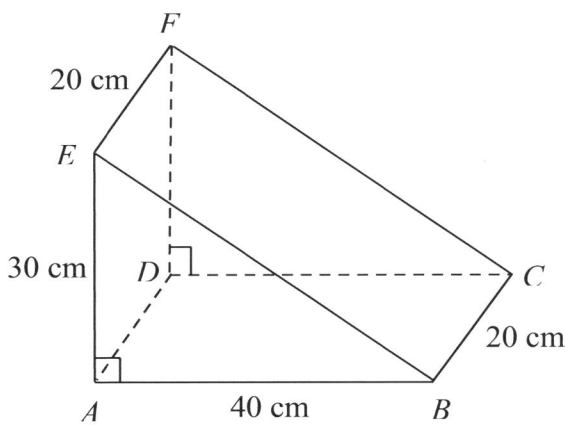

....
....
....
....
....
....

Answer……………………………….   (4 marks)

23 *OAB* is a triangle. *M* is the point on *AB* so that *AM*:*MB* = 3:1

$\overrightarrow{OA} = \mathbf{x}$, $\overrightarrow{AB} = \mathbf{y}$.

Work out the vector of $\overrightarrow{OM}$

Give your answer in terms of **x** and **y**.

....
....
....
....

Answer……………………………….   (4 marks)

24 There are 7 blue marbles and 3 red marbles in a bag. Two marbles are taken at random from the bag.

24(a) Calculate, as an exactly fraction, the probability that two marbles are different colour.

Answer……………………………. (3 marks)

24(b) Calculate, as an exactly fraction, the probability that both marbles are the same colour.

Answer……………………………. (3 marks)

25 The scatter graph shows the heights of boys at different ages.

25(a) Draw a line of best fit on the scatter graph.

(3 marks)

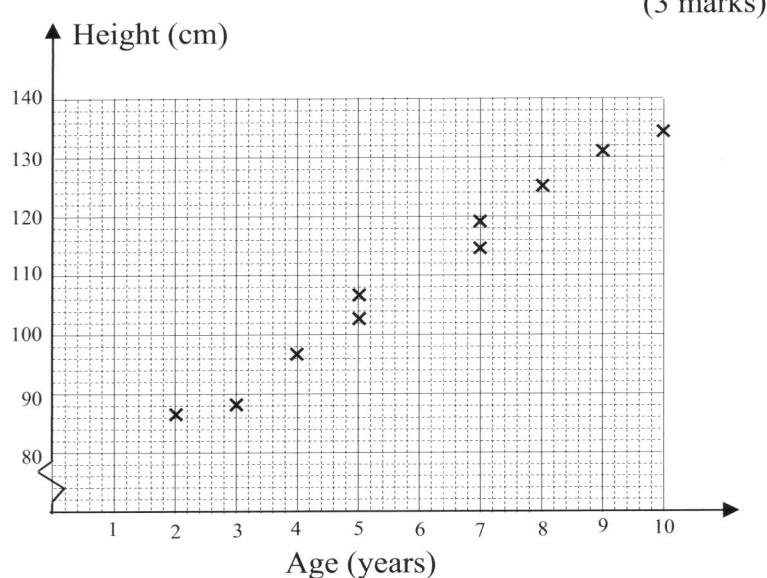

25(b) Estimate the height of a six year old.

....

....

Answer……………………….   (3 marks)

Paper 3 (Non-Calculator)

Materials

For this paper you must have:
- mathematical instruments

You **must** not use a calculator

Time allowed

1 hour 30 minutes.

Instructions
- Use black ink or black ball-point pen. Draw diagrams in pencil.
- Answer all questions.
- You must answer the questions in the space provided. Do not write outside the box around each page or on blank pages.
- Do all rough work in this book. Cross through any work that you do not want to be marked.
- In all calculations, show clearly how you work out your answer.

Information
- The marks for questions are shown in brackets.
- The maximum mark is 80.

Advice
- Read each question carefully before you start to answer it.
- Keep an eye on the time.
- Try to answer every question.
- Check your answers if you have time at the end.

1   One of these graphs is a sketch of $y = -\dfrac{x^2 + x - 2}{2}$

Which one?

Circle the correct letter.

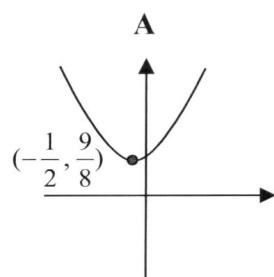

A

$(-\dfrac{1}{2}, \dfrac{9}{8})$

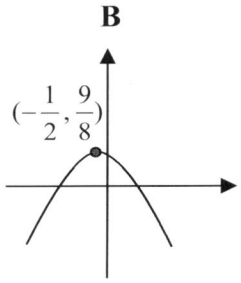

B

$(-\dfrac{1}{2}, \dfrac{9}{8})$

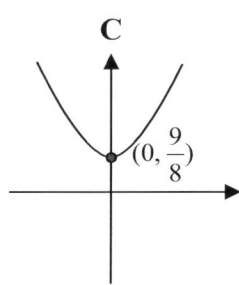

C

$(0, \dfrac{9}{8})$

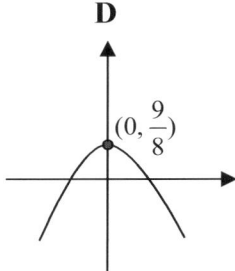

D

$(0, \dfrac{9}{8})$

………………………………………………………………………………………………
………………………………………………………………………………………………

(2 marks)

2   What is 950 million in standard form?

Circle your answer.

950×10^6 95×10^7 9.5×10^8 0.95×10^9 9.5×10^9 9.5×10^{10}

………………………………………………………………………………………………
………………………………………………………………………………………………

(2 marks)

3   Average speed = $\frac{\text{distance}}{\text{time}}$

If the distance is doubled and the time is halved, what happens to the average speed?

Circle your answer.

×2   ×4   no change   ÷2   ÷4

....

....

(2 marks)

4   The first four terms of a geometric progression are

2   8   32   128

Work out an expression, in terms of *n*, for the *n*th term.

....

....

....

....

....

....

Answer……………………………….   (3 marks)

5   Triangle **A** and triangle **B** are similar.

Triangle **A** has a circumference of 150 cm

Triangle **B** has a circumference of 30 cm

Triangle **B** has an area of 40 cm^2

Circle your answer for the area of triangle **A**.

200 cm^2 400 cm^2 1000 cm^2 2000 cm^2

....

....

....

....

....

....

Answer……………………………….   (3 marks)

6   Circle the calculation that decreases 400 by 7%

   400×0.07 400×0.93 400×0.3 400×0.7

   (2 marks)

7   Calculate $27^{-\frac{1}{3}}$.

   Circle your answer.

   3 $\frac{1}{3}$ -3 $-\frac{1}{3}$

   (2 marks)

8   Simplify $\dfrac{\sqrt{2^5}}{(\sqrt{2})^3}$

   Answer……………………….   (2 marks)

9   Circle the expression that is equivalent to $(2a^3 b^4)^3$

   $8a^9 b^{12}$ $8a^3 b^7$ $8a^6 b^7$ $6a^6 b^7$

   (2 marks)

10 Solve $x^3 = x(2x+3)$

    Answer……………………………… (3 marks)

11 Solve $\sqrt{12} + \sqrt{48} = \sqrt{27} + \sqrt{x}$

    Answer……………………………… (3 marks)

12 Here are three numbers written in standard form.

    Arrange these numbers in order of size.

    Start with the smallest number.

    3.5×10^{-7} 7.5×10^{-8} 2.5×10^{-6}

    Answer   …………………, ……………………, ……………………..
    (2 marks)

13 Factorise fully $(x^2 - 16) - (x+4)^2 + (x+4)(x+1)$

    Answer……………………………… (3 marks)

14 Expand and simplify $(3x + 4y)(4x - 3y)$

    Answer……………………………… (3 marks)

15 Write as a single fraction $\dfrac{6}{x^2-9} + \dfrac{1}{x+3}$

Give your answer in its simplest form.

Answer……………………………   (3 marks)

16 Simplify $\dfrac{\cos 45° + \sin 30°}{\tan 60°}$

Give your answer in the form $\dfrac{\sqrt{a}+\sqrt{b}}{c}$, where a, b and c are integers.

Answer……………………………   (3 marks)

17 $0.0\dot{3} = \dfrac{1}{30}$

Use this fact to show that $0.1\dot{3} = \dfrac{2}{15}$

(3 marks)

18   y is inversely proportional to x.

Complete the table.

x	3	2	
y		6	24

(3 marks)

19   Which of these represents the shaded region?

Circle your answer.

$A \cup B'$ A' $A \cap B'$ B'

(2 marks)

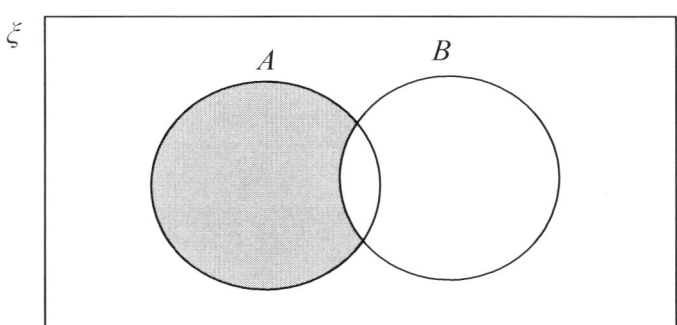

20 Here is a triangle.

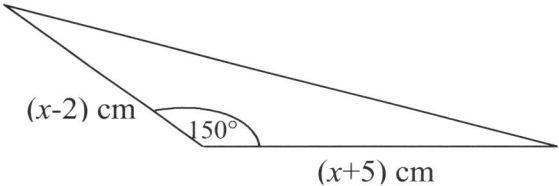

20(a) Show the area of the triangle is $\dfrac{x^2 + 3x - 10}{4}$ cm²

....
....
....
....
....

(4 marks)

20(b) The area of the triangle is greater than 11 cm².

Work out the range of the possible values of x

Give your answer as an inequality.

....
....
....
....
....
....

Answer………………………………. (3 marks)

21   There are

   8 different sandwiches

   5 different drinks

   and

   3 different snacks.

> **Meal Deal**
> Choose one sandwich, one drink and one snack

21(a)   How many different Meal Deal combinations are there?

....

....

....

   Answer……………………….   (4 marks)

21 (b)   Two of the sandwiches have cheese in them.

   Three of the drinks are fizzy.

   Emma picks a Meal Deal at random.

   Work out the probability that the sandwich has cheese in it and the drink is fizzy.

   Give your answer as a fraction in its simplest form.

....

....

....

....

....

....

....

....

   Answer……………………….   (4 marks)

22 The sketch shows part of a circle, and a line $y = -2x + 6$. The line passes the centre of the circle. The circle intersects the y-axis at points A and B.

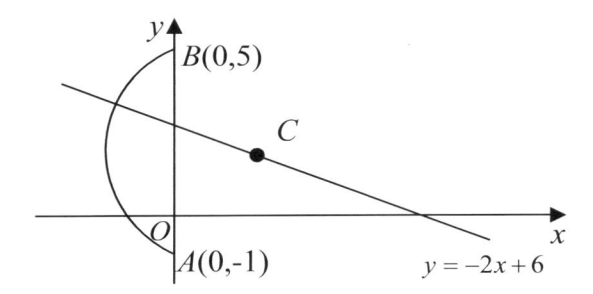

Work out the equation of the circle.

....

....

....

....

....

....

....

....

....

....

....

Answer..   (5 marks)

23 The diagram shows the graph of $y = \cos x$ for $0° \leq x \leq 360°$

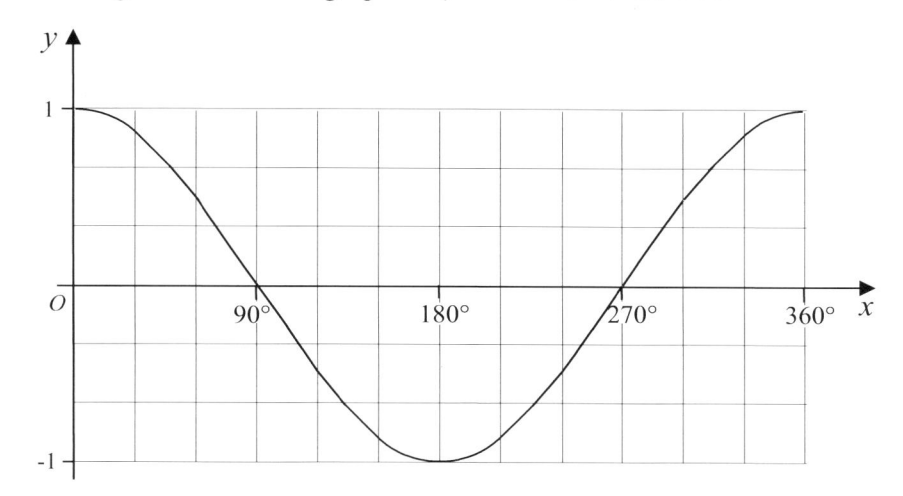

On the grid above, sketch the graph of $y = \cos(x + 60°)$ for $0° \leq x \leq 360°$

....
....
....
....
....

(4 marks)

24 The table gives information about the areas of some farms in France.

Area (A hectares)	Frequency
$0 < A \leq 20$	50
$20 < A \leq 50$	90
$50 < A \leq 100$	120
$100 < A \leq 300$	180

On the grid, draw a histogram to show this information.

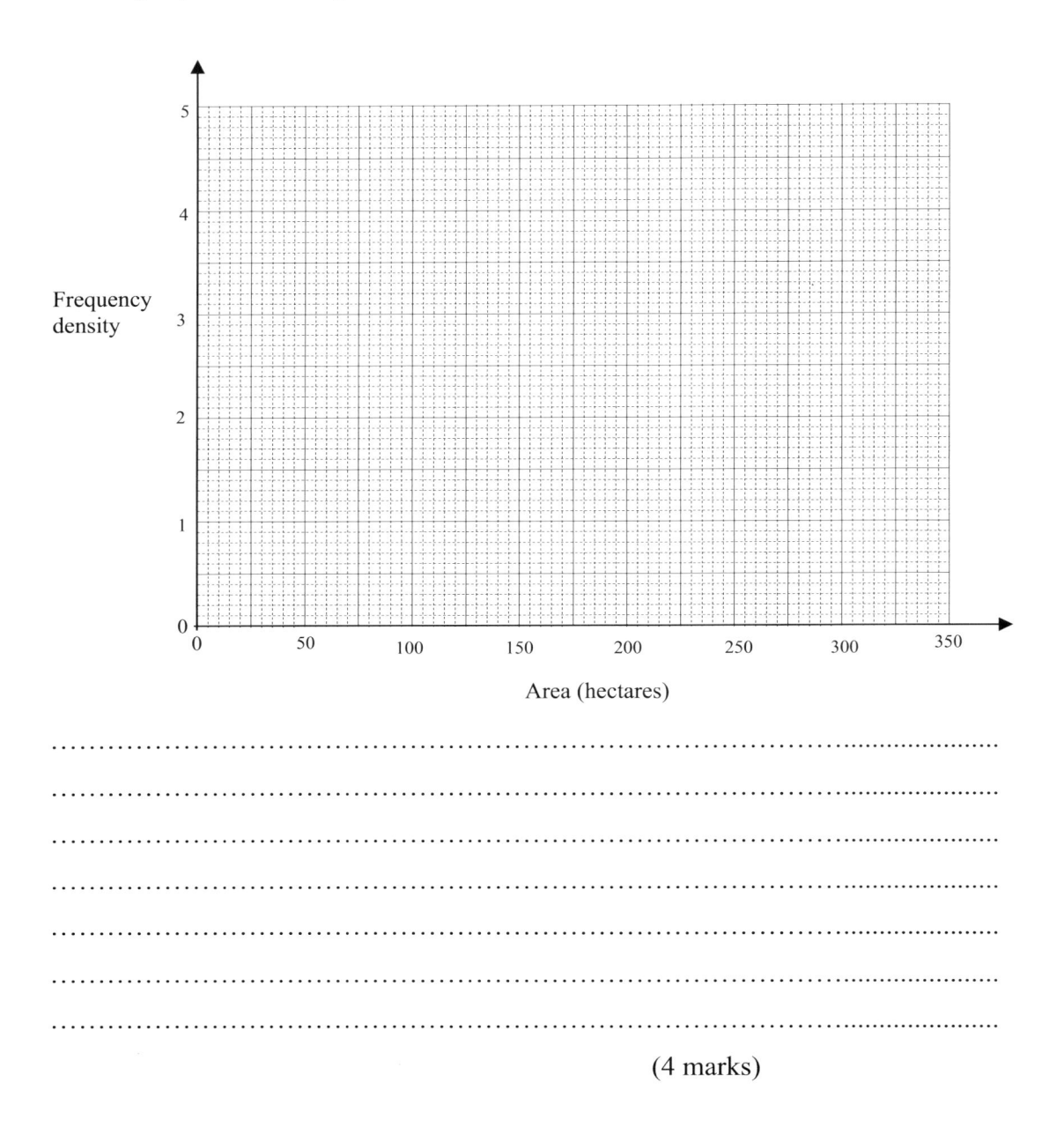

Frequency density

Area (hectares)

....
....
....
....
....
....
....

(4 marks)

25 The table shows information about the number of fish caught by 29 people in a club in one day.

Jack is one of the 29 people in the club.

Number of fish	Frequency
0	2
1	6
2	10
3	8
5	2
8	1

The number of fish caught by him was the same as the median number of fish caught for his club.

Work out the number of fish caught by him.

....

....

....

....

....

Answer……………………….   (4 marks)

Paper 4 (Non-Calculator)

Materials
For this paper you must have:
- mathematical instruments

You **must** not use a calculator

Time allowed
1 hour 30 minutes.

Instructions
- Use black ink or black ball-point pen. Draw diagrams in pencil.
- Answer all questions.
- You must answer the questions in the space provided. Do not write outside the box around each page or on blank pages.
- Do all rough work in this book. Cross through any work that you do not want to be marked.
- In all calculations, show clearly how you work out your answer.

Information
- The marks for questions are shown in brackets.
- The maximum mark is 80.

Advice
- Read each question carefully before you start to answer it.
- Keep an eye on the time.
- Try to answer every question.
- Check your answers if you have time at the end.

1 Circle the number that is closest in value to $\frac{9.999}{0.0499}$

   2   20   200   2000

   ....
   ....
   (2 marks)

2 Below are three sequences:

   A: Quadratic sequence;   B: Arithmetic sequence;

   C: Geometric progression

   Which sequence does each of the three below belong to? Circle your answer.

2(a) 2   6   10   14   ...   A   B   C

2(b) 2   8   32   128   ...   A   B   C

2(c) 101   104   109   116   ...   A   B   C

   ....
   ....
   ....
   ....
   ....
   ....
   (3 marks)

3 Solid **A** and Solid **B** are mathematically similar.

   Solid **A** has a volume of 8000 cm^3

   Solid **B** has a volume of 1000 cm^3

   Solid **A** has surface area 4000 cm^2

   Circle your answer for the surface area of solid **B**.

   1000 cm^2 2000 cm^2 4000 cm^2 8000 cm^2

   ....
   ....
   ....
   (2 marks)

7

41

4   Volume = $\frac{\text{mass}}{\text{density}}$

The mass of solid A is 9 times the mass of solid B.

The density of solid A is 3 times the density of solid B.

Complete the sentence.

The volume of solid A is …………………………..times the volume of solid B.

(2 marks)

5   P is directly proportional to Q^2 where $Q > 0$. $P = 400$ when $Q = 4$.

5(a)   Find a formula for P in terms of Q.

Answer…………………………….   (2 marks)

5(b)   Find the value of Q when $P = 100$.

Answer…………………………….   (2 marks)

6(a)   Work out $2\frac{1}{6} + 1\frac{3}{4}$

Answer…………………………….   (2 marks)

6(b) Work out $1\frac{3}{5} \div \frac{4}{7}$.

Give your answer as a mixed number in its simplest form.

Answer……………………………… (2 marks)

7   60% of p = 20% of q.

Work out an expression of p, as a fraction in its simplest form, in terms of q.

Answer……………………………… (2 marks)

8   Factorise fully $4x^4 - 16x^2$.

Answer……………………………… (2 marks)

9   $x:y = 3:2$ and $y:z = 5:8$

Work out $x:y:z$

Give your answer in its simplest form.

Answer……………………………… (2 marks)

10 Solve $4^{\frac{1}{8}} \times 2^x = 8^{\frac{3}{4}}$

....
....
....
....

Answer……………………….   (2 marks)

11 Solve $\dfrac{2}{2x+1} + \dfrac{1}{4x^2-1} = 1$

....
....
....
....
....
....

Answer……………………….   (2 marks)

12 Write 2.3×10^{-4} as an ordinary number.

Circle your answer.

0.00023   0.0023   0.023   0.023

(1 mark)

13 Simplify $\sqrt{128} - \sqrt{98}$

....
....
....
....

Answer……………………….   (2 marks)

14   Write $(2\sqrt{3}+3\sqrt{2})^2$ in the form $p+q\sqrt{6}$, where p and q are integers.

....
....
....
....

          Answer………………………….   (2 marks)

15   Using algebra, prove that $\dfrac{0.\dot{3}\dot{6}}{0.\dot{3}}$ is equal in value to $1\dfrac{1}{11}$

....
....
....
....
....
....
....
....

                                          (3 marks)

16   Prove that $\dfrac{\tan 60° + \tan 45°}{\sin 60° + \sin 30°}$ is an integer.

....
....
....
....
....
....

                                          (3 marks)

8

45

17   x kg = y lbs

Write a formula for y in terms of x, by using 5 kg=11 lbs.

....
....
....
....
....
....

　　　　　Answer……………………….   (3 marks)

18   Here is a triangle.

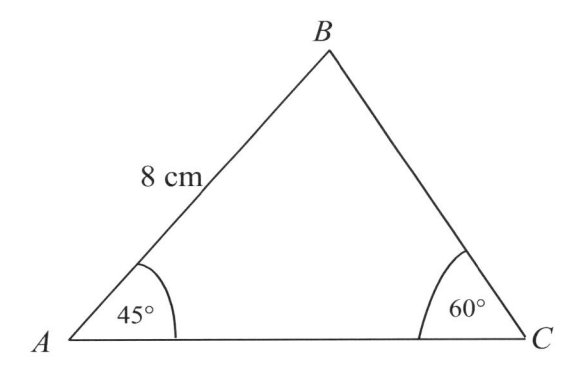

Triangle ABC with B at top, A at bottom-left, C at bottom-right. AB = 8 cm, angle A = 45°, angle C = 60°.

Work out the length of *BC*.

....
....
....
....
....
....

　　　　　Answer……………………….   (3 marks)

19 *ABC* is an isosceles triangle. *AC* is a tangent to the circle.

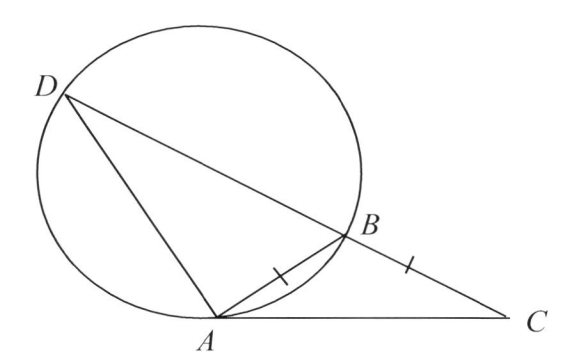

Prove that *ACD* is an isosceles triangle.

....
....
....
....
....
....

(3 marks)

20 The distance-time graph shows information about part of a car journey.

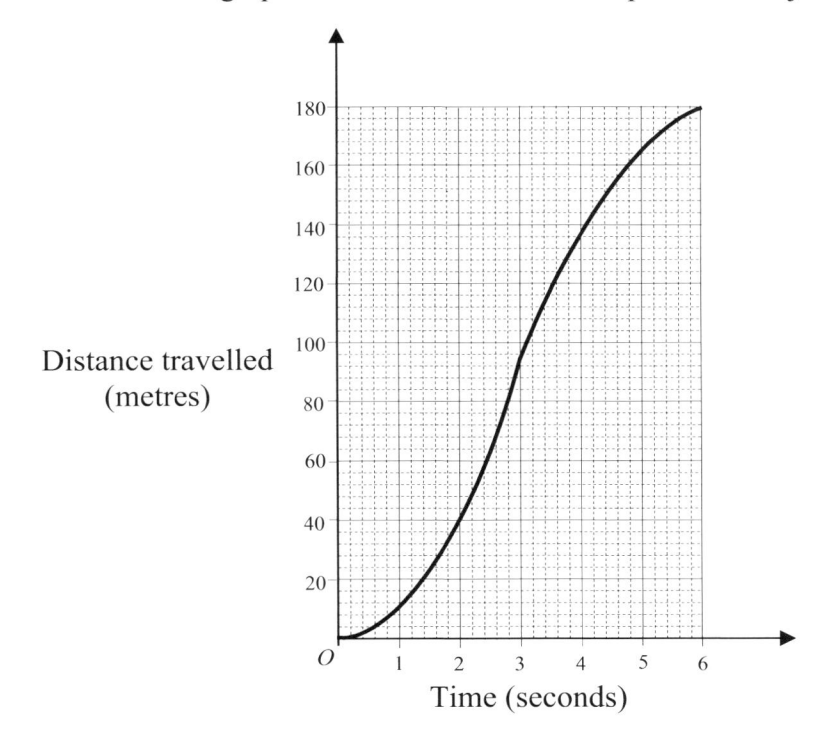

20(a) Work out the average speed during the 6 seconds.

....
....
....
....
....
....

Answer................................ (3 marks)

20(b) Use the graph to estimate the speed of the car at time 2 seconds.

Give your answer to 1 decimal place.

....
....
....
....
....
....

Answer................................ (3 marks)

21 A line passes through (3,4) and (6,10).

Work out the equation of the line.

....
....
....
....
....

Answer................................ (2 marks)

22   The graph shows two lines A and B.

The equation of line B is $y = \frac{1}{2}x + \frac{7}{2}$. The two lines are perpendicular each other and intersect at (1,4)

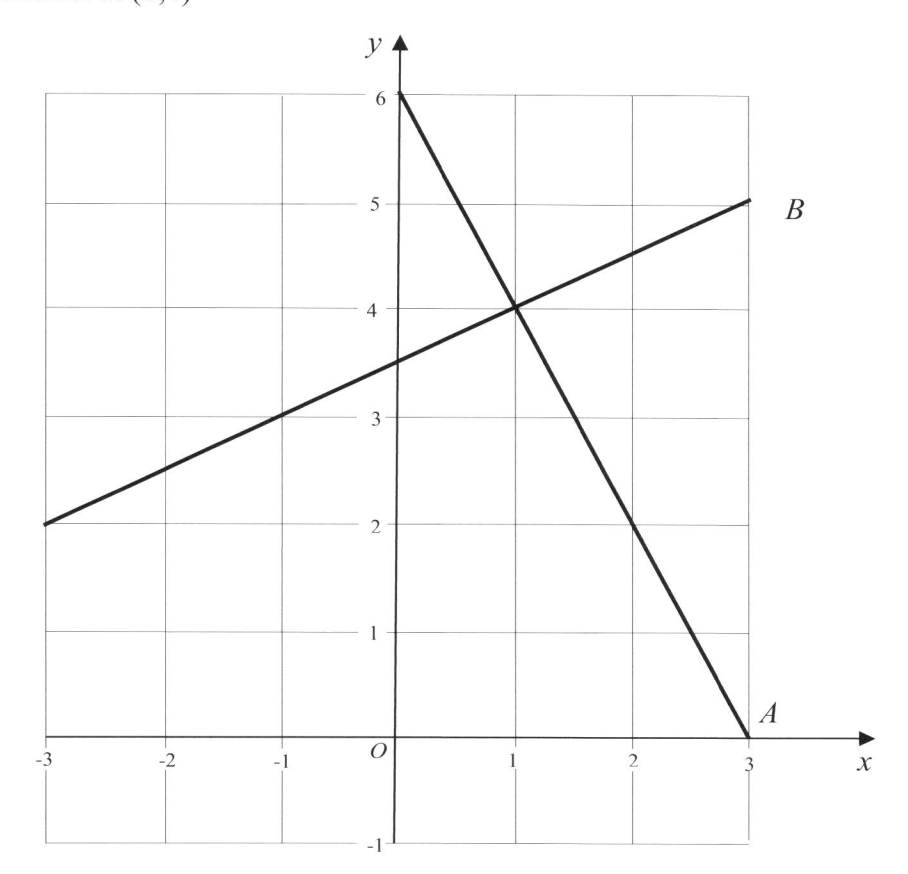

Work out the equation of line A.

....

....

....

....

....

Answer……………………….   (3 marks)

23(a) On the diagram, draw the image of Shape A when it is reflected in the x-axis.

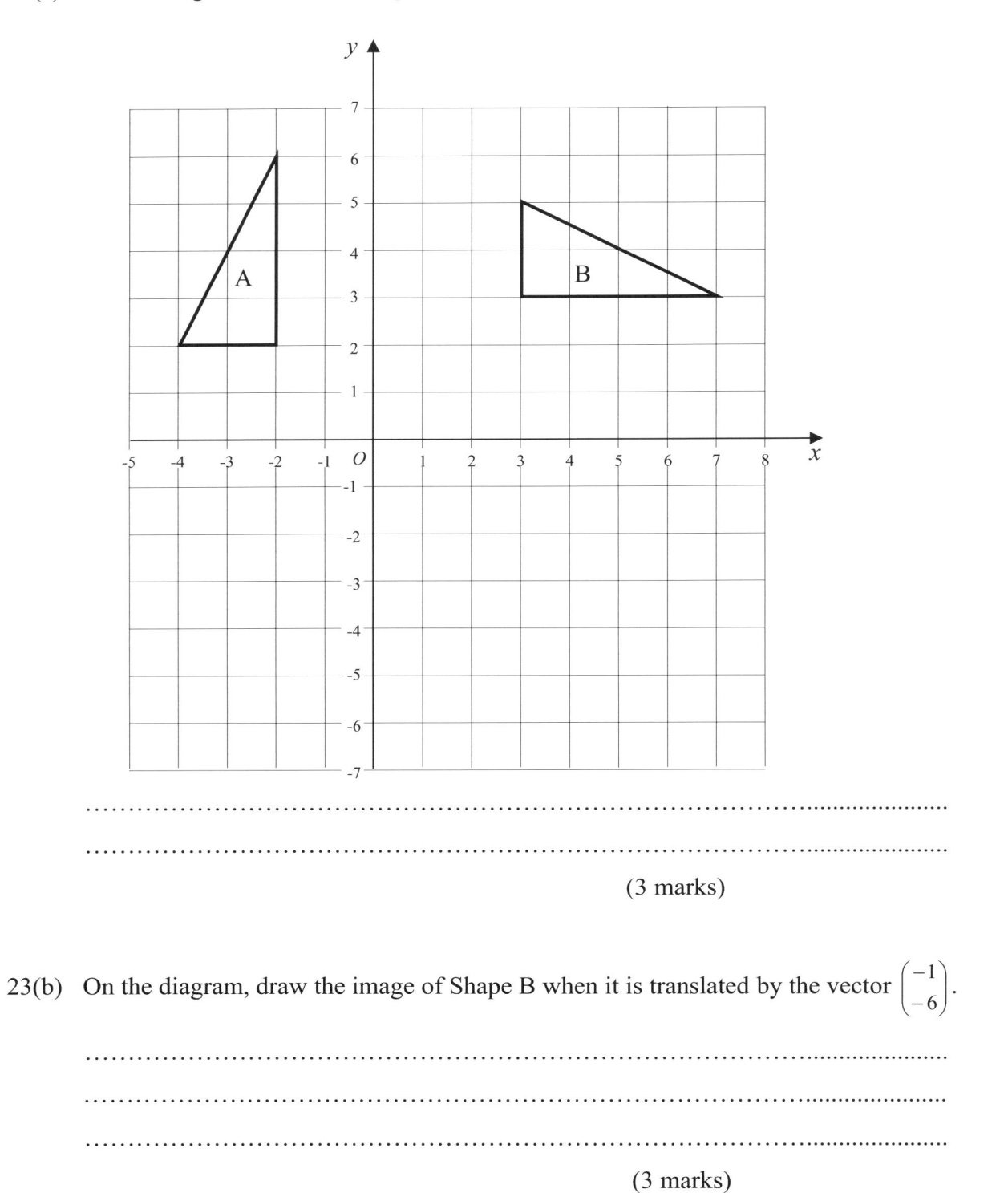

....
....
(3 marks)

23(b) On the diagram, draw the image of Shape B when it is translated by the vector $\begin{pmatrix} -1 \\ -6 \end{pmatrix}$.

....
....
....
(3 marks)

23(c) Describe fully the single transformation which will map Shape A onto Shape B.

....
(3 marks)

24 There are 9 counters in a bag.

There is a number on each counter.

① ① ② ② ② ③ ③ ③ ③

Jack takes at random 2 counters from the bag.

He adds together the numbers on the 2 counters to get his Total.

24(a) Complete and fully label the probability tree diagram to show the possible outcome.

First counter   Second counter

$\frac{2}{9}$ 1

2

3

....
....
....
....

(3 marks)

24(b) Work out the probability that his Total is greater than 3.

Give your answer as a fraction in its simplest form.

....
....
....
....

Answer................................. (2 marks)

25   The cumulative frequency table shows information about the height of 50 men.

Height (h cm)	Cumulative frequency
$150 < h \leq 160$	5
$150 < h \leq 170$	15
$150 < h \leq 180$	35
$150 < h \leq 190$	45
$150 < h \leq 200$	50

25(a)   On the grid, draw a cumulative frequency graph for the table.

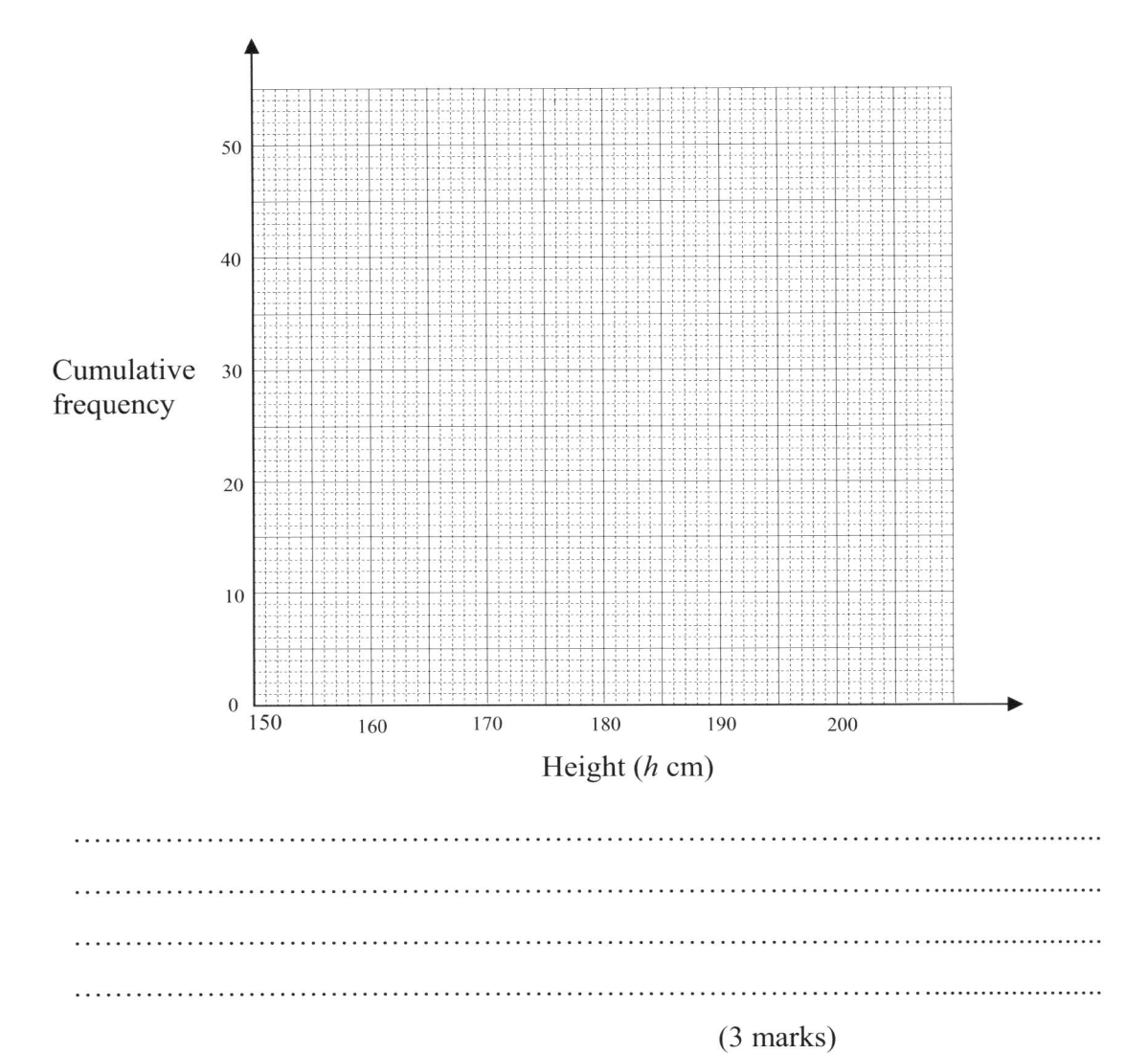

....
....
....
....

(3 marks)

3

25(b) Use your graph to find an estimate for the median height of the 50 men.

....

....

....

Answer................................ (3 marks)

25(c) Use your graph to find an estimate for the number of the men who are taller than 185 cm.

....

....

....

....

Answer................................ (2 marks)

Paper 1 solutions

1   Circle the area that is the same as 20 cm²

   0.2 mm²   2 mm²   200 mm²   2000 mm²

   Answer   2000 mm²   (2 marks)

2   Which of these represents the shaded region?

   Circle your answer.

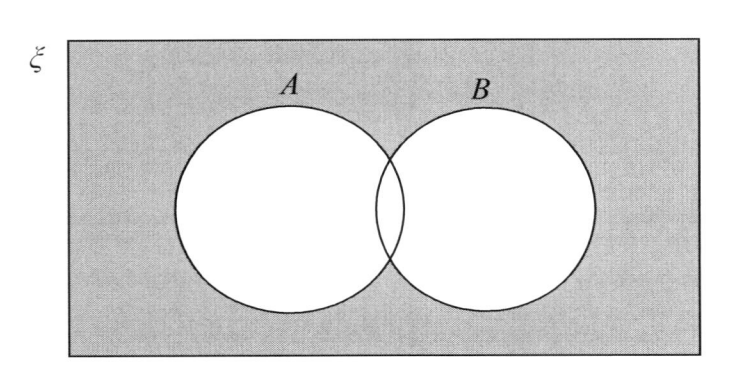

   $(A \cup B)'$ A' $(A \cap B)'$ B'

   Answer $(A \cup B)'$ (2 marks)

4   Emma invests £5000 for 5 years. The investment gets compound interest of 5% per annum.

   Which of these calculates how much the investment is worth at the end of 5 years?

   Circle your answer.

   $5000 \times (1+5\%)^5$ $5000 \times (5\%)^5$ $5000 \times (1+5 \times 5\%)$ $5000 \times (5 \times 5\%)$

   Answer $5000 \times (1+5\%)^5$ (2 marks)

4   Write $0.1\dot{3}\dot{6}$ as a fraction in its simplest form.

   $x = 0.1\dot{3}\dot{6}$ (1)

   $100x = 13.6\dot{3}\dot{6}$ (2)

   Eq. (2)-Eq. (1) $\Rightarrow 99x = 13.5 \Rightarrow x = \dfrac{3}{22}$

   Answer $\dfrac{3}{22}$ (3 marks)

9

54

5   The first four terms of an arithmetic sequence are

     7   13   19   25

     Work out an expression, in terms of *n*, for the *n*th term.

     $a_n = a_1 + (n-1)d$

     $\Rightarrow a_2 = a_1 + d \Rightarrow d = a_2 - a_1 \Rightarrow d = 13 - 7 = 6$, where $n = 2$.

     $\therefore \ a_n = 7 + 6(n-1) = 6n + 1$

     Answer $6n+1$ (3 marks)

6   Expand and simplify $(2+\sqrt{3})(3-\sqrt{3})$

     Give your answer in the form $a+b\sqrt{3}$, where *a* and *b* are integers.

     Show your working clearly.

     $(2+\sqrt{3})(3-\sqrt{3}) = (2+\sqrt{3})(1+2-\sqrt{3}) = (2+\sqrt{3})+(2+\sqrt{3})(2-\sqrt{3}) = (2+\sqrt{3})+1 = 3+\sqrt{3}$

     Answer $3+\sqrt{3}$ (2 marks)

7   Factorise fully $4x^2 - 25$

     $4x^2 - 25 = (2x)^2 - 5^2 = (2x-5)(2x+5)$

     Answer $(2x-5)(2x+5)$ (2 marks)

8   Simplify the expression $(3x^2 y^3)^3$

     $(3x^2 y^3)^3 = 3^3 x^{2 \times 3} y^{3 \times 3} = 27 x^6 y^9$

     Answer $27x^6 y^9$ (2 marks)

9   Solve the equation $x^2 - 2x - 2 = 0$

     Give your answer in the form $a \pm \sqrt{b}$, where *a* and *b* are integers.

     $x = \dfrac{2 \pm \sqrt{4 + 4 \times 2}}{2} = 1 \pm \sqrt{3}$

     Answer $1 \pm \sqrt{3}$ (2 marks)

11

10 $a - 2b < 12$ and $a + b = 6$

Work out the range of possible values of b.

Give your answer as an inequality.

$a + b = 6 \Rightarrow a = 6 - b$

$a - 2b < 12 \Rightarrow 6 - b - 2b < 12 \Rightarrow b > -2$

Answer $b > -2$ (3 marks)

11 50% of p = 20% of q.

Work out p as a percentage of q.

$50\% p = 20\% q \Rightarrow p = \dfrac{2}{5} q \Rightarrow p = 40\% q$

Answer $p = 40\% q$ (2 marks)

12 Without using a calculator, evaluate $\dfrac{\sqrt{32} + \sqrt{50}}{\sqrt{18}}$

Show all your working.

$\dfrac{\sqrt{32} + \sqrt{50}}{\sqrt{18}} = \dfrac{4\sqrt{2} + 5\sqrt{2}}{3\sqrt{2}} = 3$

Answer 3 (2 marks)

13 Find an approximate value for $\dfrac{\sqrt{9.115} \times 10^5}{5.997 \times 10^{-4}}$

Give your answer in standard form.

$\dfrac{\sqrt{9.115} \times 10^5}{5.997 \times 10^{-4}} \approx \dfrac{3 \times 10^5}{6 \times 10^{-4}} = 0.5 \times 10^9 = 5 \times 10^8$

Answer 5×10^8 (2 marks)

15 Work out $2\dfrac{2}{3} \times 1\dfrac{5}{7}$.

Give your answer as a mixed number in its simplest form.

$2\dfrac{2}{3} \times 1\dfrac{5}{7} = \dfrac{8}{\cancel{3}_1} \times \dfrac{\cancel{12}^4}{7} = \dfrac{32}{7} = 4\dfrac{4}{7}$

Answer $4\dfrac{4}{7}$ (2 marks)

15   Write as a single power of x

$$\left(\frac{x^{\frac{1}{3}} \times x^{\frac{5}{3}}}{x}\right)^2$$

$$\left(\frac{x^{\frac{1}{3}} \times x^{\frac{5}{3}}}{x}\right)^2 = \left(x^{\frac{1}{3}+\frac{5}{3}-1}\right)^2 = (x^1)^2 = x^{1 \times 2} = x^2$$

Answer x^2 (2 marks)

16   Simplify $\dfrac{\sin 60° + \tan 30°}{\sin 45°}$

Give your answer in the form $\dfrac{a}{b}\sqrt{c}$, where a, b and c are integers

$$\frac{\sin 60° + \tan 30°}{\sin 45°} = \frac{\frac{\sqrt{3}}{2}+\frac{\sqrt{3}}{3}}{\frac{\sqrt{2}}{2}} = \frac{(\frac{\sqrt{3}}{2}+\frac{\sqrt{3}}{3}) \times \sqrt{2}}{\frac{\sqrt{2}}{2} \times \sqrt{2}} = \frac{\frac{5\sqrt{3}}{6} \times \sqrt{2}}{\frac{2}{2}} = \frac{5}{6}\sqrt{6}$$

Answer $\dfrac{5}{6}\sqrt{6}$ (3 marks)

17   a, b, c and d are consecutive integers.

Prove that $ab + cd$ is always even.

$b = a+1$, $c = a+2$, $d = a+2$

$ab + cd = a(a+1) + (a+2)(a+3) = a^2 + a + a^2 + 5a + 6 = 2(a^2 + 3a + 3)$

$\therefore ab + cd$ is always even.

(3 marks)

18 The square *ABCD* is drawn inside the regular octagon *ABEFGHIJ*. They share side *AB*.

Work out the value of *x*.

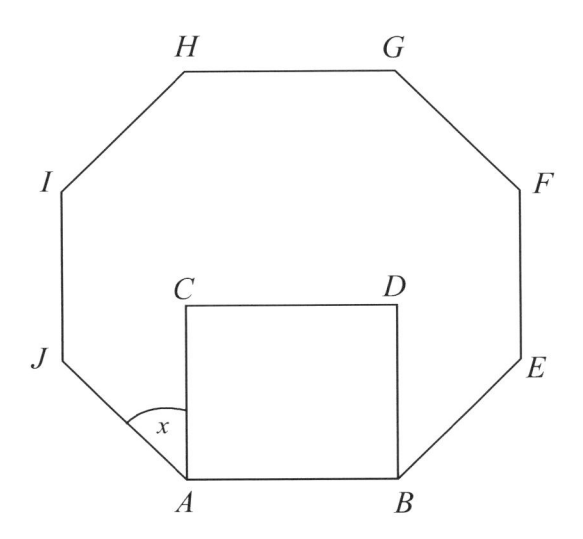

$\angle CAB = 90°$, $\angle JAB = \dfrac{(8-2)}{8} \times 180° = 135°$

$x = \angle JAB - \angle CAB = 135° - 90° = 45°$

Answer   45°   (4 marks)

19 *ABCD* is a quadrilateral.

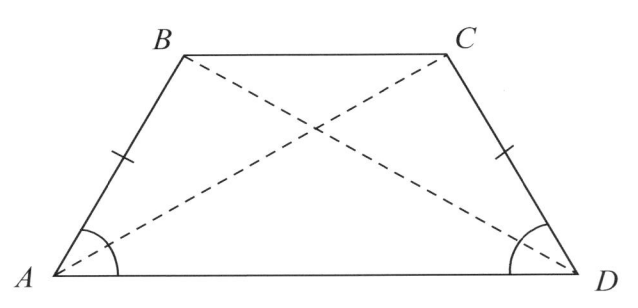

AB = *CD*.

$\angle BAD = \angle ADC$.

Prove that triangle *ABD* is congruent to triangle *DAC*.

AB = *CD*

$\angle BAD = \angle ADC$

Triangle *ABD* and triangle *DAC* share the same side *AD*

∴ Triangle *ABD* is congruent to triangle *DAC* (SAS).

(4 marks)

20   The equation of the circle is $x^2 - 10x + y^2 - 4y + 13 = 0$.

20(a)   Work out the coordinates of the centre of the circle.

$x^2 - 10x + y^2 - 4y + 13 = 0 \Rightarrow (x-5)^2 - 25 + (y-2)^2 - 4 + 13 = 0 \Rightarrow (x-5)^2 + (y-2)^2 = 16$

The coordinates of the centre of the circle are (5,2).

Answer   (5,2)   (3 marks)

20(b)   Work out the diameter of the circle.

The radius of the circle is 4 units from part (a) above.

The diameter of the circle is 8 units.

Answer   8 units   (3 marks)

21   *P*(2,4) is a point on a circle, centre *O*.

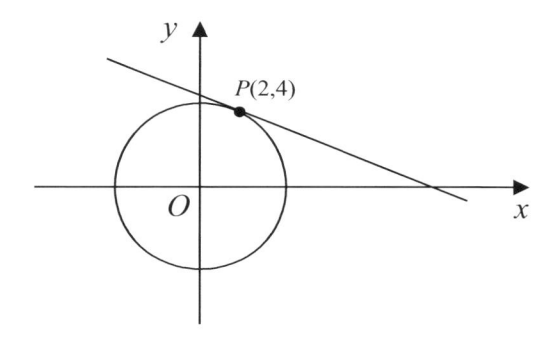

21(a)   Work out the equation of the circle.

The radius of the circle is $\sqrt{P_x^2 + P_y^2} = \sqrt{2^2 + 4^2} = \sqrt{20}$

The equation of the circle is $x^2 + y^2 = 20$

Answer $x^2 + y^2 = 20$ (3 marks)

21(b) Work out the equation of the tangent to the circle at P.

Give your answer in the form $y = mx + c$

The gradient of OP is $\dfrac{P_y}{P_x} = \dfrac{4}{2} = 2$

The gradient of the tangent is $-\dfrac{1}{2}$

The equation of the tangent to the circle at P is $y - 4 = -\dfrac{1}{2}(x - 2) \Rightarrow$

$y = -\dfrac{1}{2}x + 5$

Answer $\quad y = -\dfrac{1}{2}x + 5 \quad$ (3 marks)

22 $\quad f(x)$ is a quadratic function.

The diagram shows part of the graph of $y = f(x)$.

Points $A(-1,0)$, $B(0,-2)$ and $C(4,0)$ lie on $y = f(x)$.

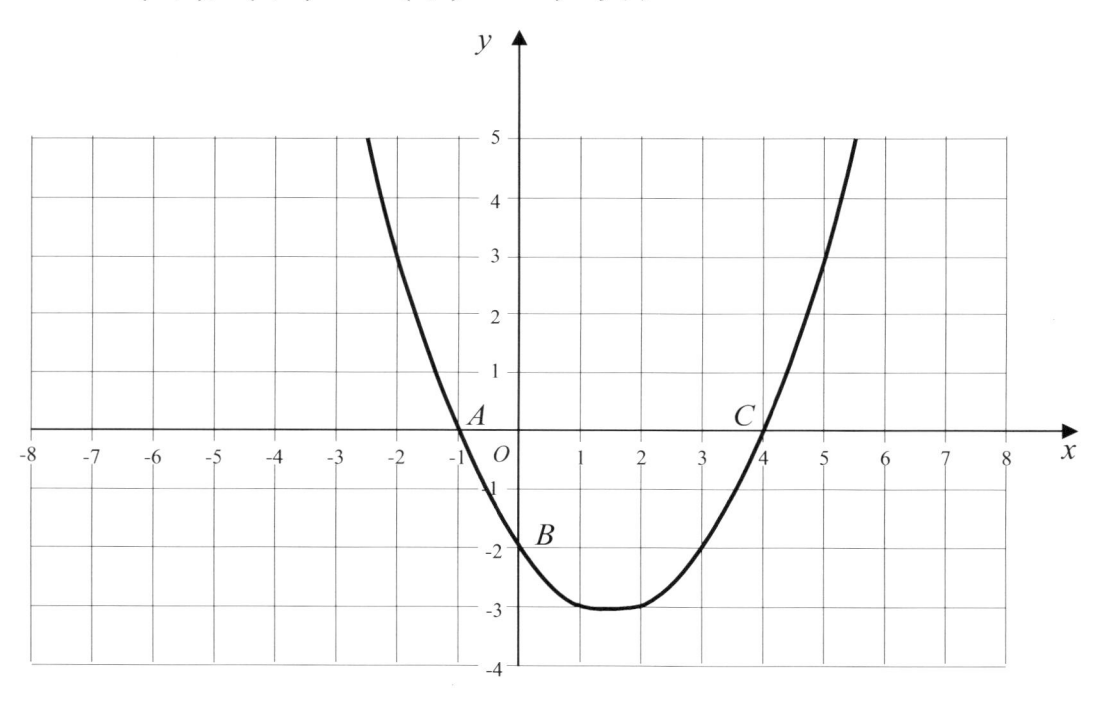

22(a) The graph of $y = f(x+4)$ represents a transformation of the graph of $y = f(x)$.

On the grid below, sketch the graph of $y = f(x+4)$.

On your graph mark clearly with crosses the images of A, B and C in the transformation.

The graph of $y = f(x+4)$ can be drawn by translating the graph of $y = f(x)$, 4 squares to the left, as shown.

In the same way, the images of A, B and C in the transformation can be drawn by translating of A, B and C, 4 squares to the left, as shown.

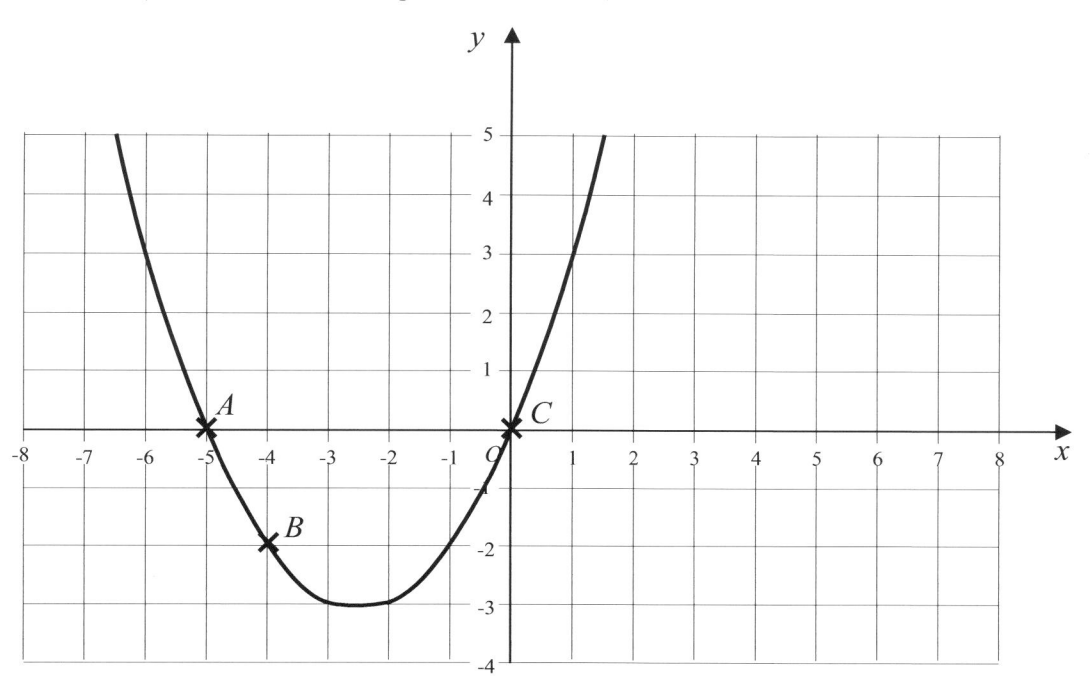

(4 marks)

22(b) The graph of $y = f(-x)$ represents another transformation of the graph of $y = f(x)$.

On the grid below, sketch of $y = f(-x)$.

On your graph mark clearly with crosses the images of A, B and C in the transformation.

The graph of $y = f(x)$ is reflected in the y-axis to give the graph of $y = f(-x)$, as shown.

In the same way, points A, B and C are reflected in the y-axis to give the images of A, B and C in the transformation, as shown.

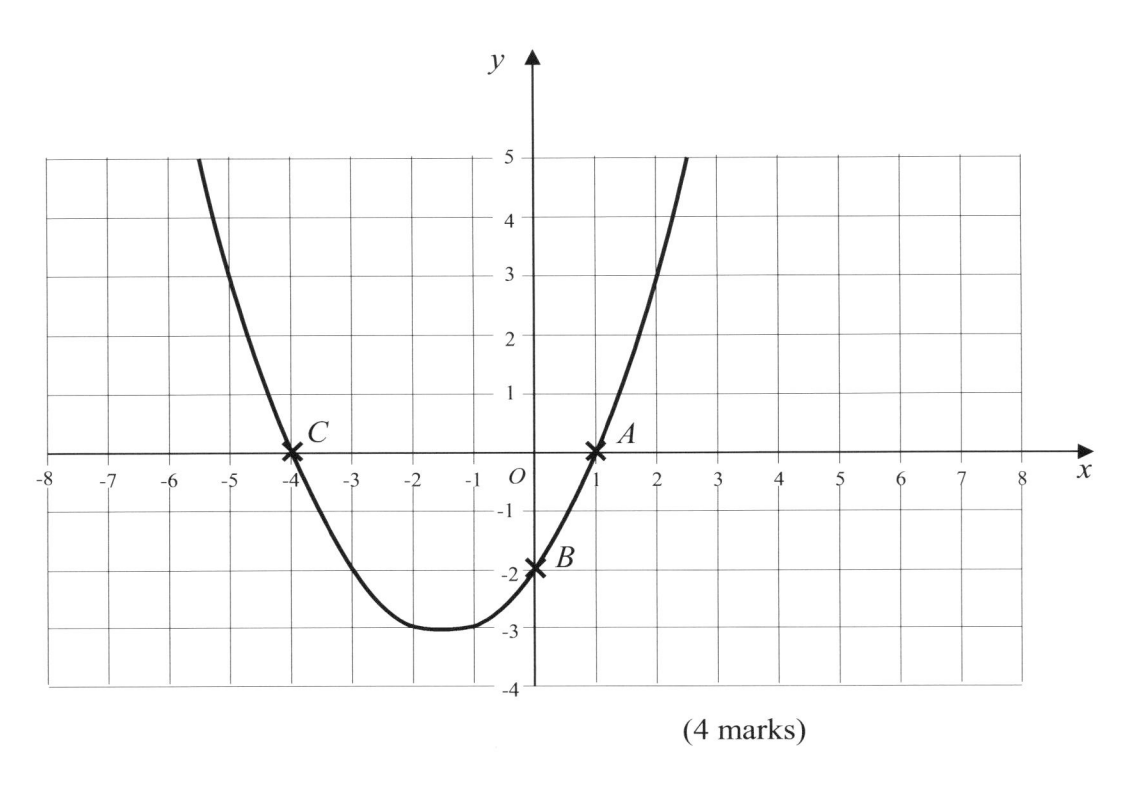

(4 marks)

23 The four candidates in an election were A, B, C and D.

The pie chart shows the proportion of votes for each candidate.

Work out the probability that a person who voted, chosen at random, voted for A.

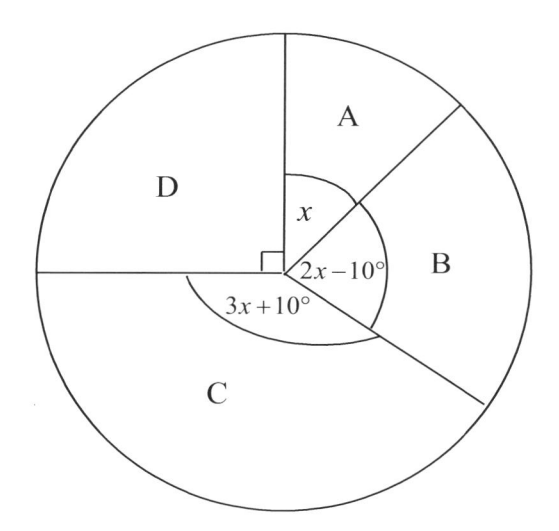

$$x + (2x - 10°) + (3x + 10°) + 90° = 360° \Rightarrow x = \frac{270°}{6} = 45°$$

The probability that a person voted for A is

$$\frac{45°}{360°} = \frac{1}{8}$$

Answer $\frac{1}{8}$ (4 marks)

24   The histogram gives information about the heights of 540 Christmas trees.

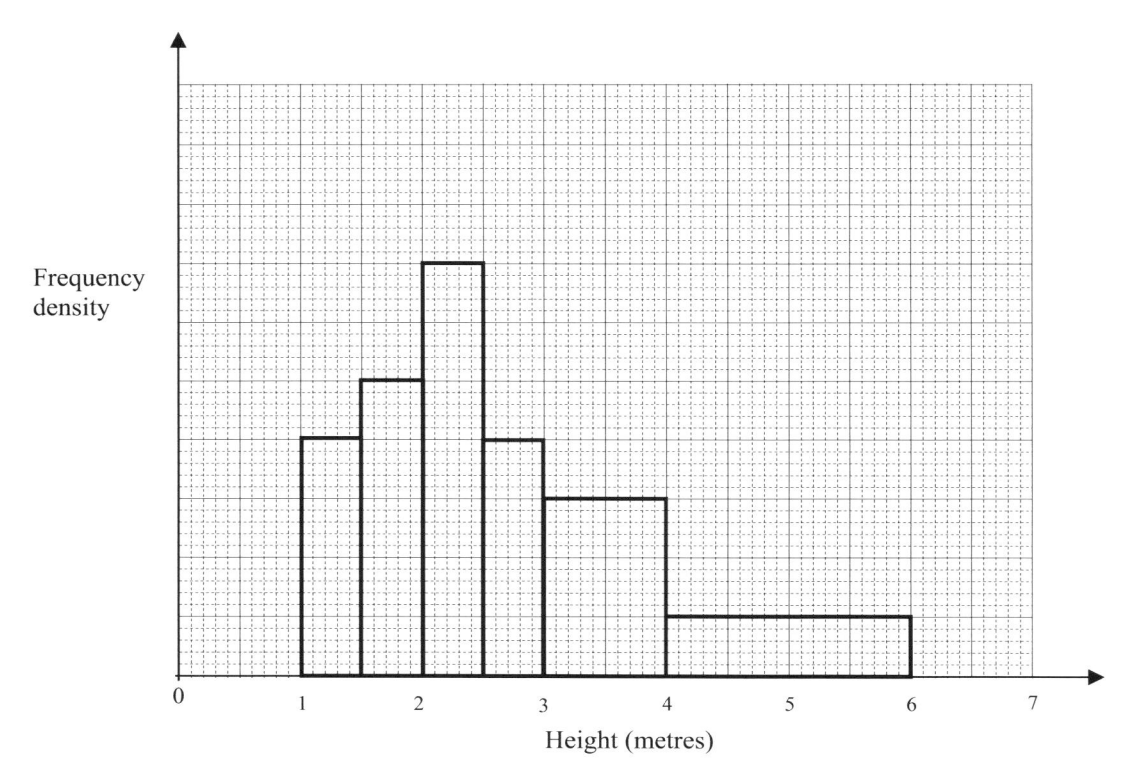

Frequency density

Height (metres)

There is no Christmas tree shorter than 1 metre.

There is no Christmas tree taller than 6 metres.

Work out an estimate for the number of Christmas trees with a height greater than 3 metres.

The estimate for the number of Christmas trees is directly proportional to the area enclosed by the histogram.

From the diagram, the area enclosed by the histogram for a height greater than 3 metres is one third of the whole area enclosed by the histogram.

The estimate for the number of Christmas trees with a height greater than 3 metres is:

$\frac{1}{3} \times 540 = 180$

Answer   180   (4 marks)

25   *OABC* is a parallelogram.

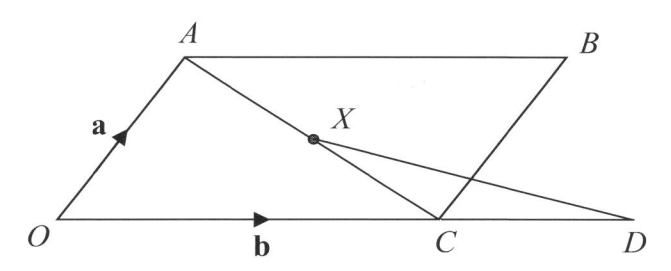

$\vec{OA} = \mathbf{a}$, $\vec{OC} = \mathbf{b}$

X is the midpoint of the line *AC*.

OCD is a straight line so that *OC*:*CD*=2:1

Work out the vector of $\vec{XD}$

Give your answer in terms of **a** and **b**.

$\vec{AC} = \vec{OC} - \vec{OA} = \mathbf{b} - \mathbf{a}$

$\vec{XC} = \dfrac{\vec{AC}}{2} = \dfrac{\mathbf{b} - \mathbf{a}}{2}$

$OC{:}CD{=}2{:}1 \Rightarrow \vec{CD} = \dfrac{\vec{OC}}{2} = \dfrac{\mathbf{b}}{2}$

$\vec{XD} = \vec{XC} + \vec{CD} = \dfrac{\mathbf{b} - \mathbf{a}}{2} + \dfrac{\mathbf{b}}{2} = \mathbf{b} - \dfrac{\mathbf{a}}{2}$

Answer $\vec{XD} = \mathbf{b} - \dfrac{\mathbf{a}}{2}$ (5 marks)

Paper 2 solutions

1 Simplify $(2^2 \times 2^3)^2$

Circle the answer.

2^{10} 2^{12} 4^{10} 4^{12}

$(2^2 \times 2^3)^2 = (2^{2+3})^2 = (2^5)^2 = 2^{5 \times 2} = 2^{10}$

Answer 2^{10} (2 marks)

3 On 1 April 2019, the cost of 5 grams of gold was £220. The cost of gold increased by 10% from 1 April 2018 to 1 April 2019.

Circle the calculation for the cost of 5 grams of gold on 1 April 2018.

$\dfrac{220}{1.10}$ 220×1.10 $220 \times (1-0.1)$ $\dfrac{220}{1.01}$

The cost of 5 grams of gold on 1 April 2018 is $\dfrac{220}{1+10\%} = \dfrac{220}{1.10}$

Answer $\dfrac{220}{1.10}$ (2 marks)

3 Circle the volume that is the same as 2.2 m³

2.2×10^3 cm³ 2.2×10^6 cm³ 2.2×10^9 cm³ 2.2×10^{12} cm³

$1 \, \text{m} = 100 \, \text{cm} \Rightarrow 1 \, \text{m}^3 = (100 \, \text{cm})^3 = 10^6 \, \text{cm}^3$

$2.2 \, \text{m}^3 = 2.2 \times 10^6 \, \text{cm}^3$

Answer 2.2×10^6 cm³   (2 marks)

4 $x : y = 3 : 4$ and z is 20% of y.

Work out $x : y : z$

Give your answer in its simplest form.

$x : y = 3 : 4 \Rightarrow x : y = 15 : 20$ (1)

$z = 20\% y \Rightarrow y : z = 100 : 20 \Rightarrow y : z = 20 : 4$ (2)

$x : y : z = 15 : 20 : 4$

Answer $15 : 20 : 4$ (2 marks)

5   Below are four equations:

Equation 1: $y = 3x - 3$; Equation 2: $y = 2x^2 + 3$

Equation 3: $3x + 6y = 12$; Equation 4: $y = 3x^3$

5(a) Match one the equations to each of the three graphs below:

Graph A Graph B Graph C

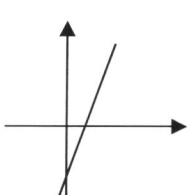

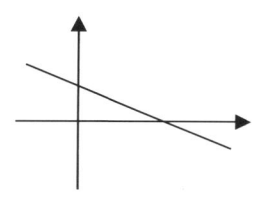

Equation 1 Equation 3 Equation 2

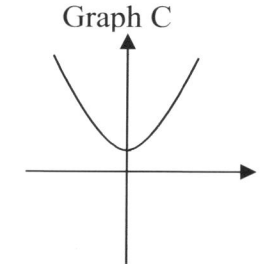

(3 marks)

5(b) Draw the graph of the remaining equation on the axes below.

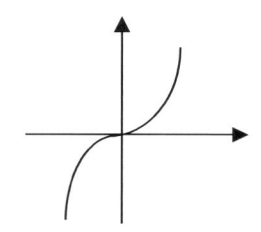

Equation 4

(2 marks)

6   Write $0.\dot{6}\dot{3}$ as a fraction in its simplest form.

$x = 0.\dot{6}\dot{3}$ (1)

$100x = 63.\dot{6}\dot{3}$ (2)

Eq. (2)-Eq. (1) $\Rightarrow 99x = 63 \Rightarrow x = \dfrac{63}{99} = \dfrac{7}{11}$

Answer $\dfrac{7}{11}$ (3 marks)

8

7   A linear sequence starts
    3   10   17   24   …

Work out an expression for the nth term.

If the nth term is $an+b$

Then the first term: $a+b=3$ (1)

The second term: $2a+b=10$ (2)

Eq. (2)-Eq. (1) $\Rightarrow a=7$, $b=-4$ from Eq. (1).

∴ The expression for the nth term is $7n-4$

    Answer $7n-4$ (3 marks)

8   Rationalise the denominator and simply fully $\dfrac{6}{3-\sqrt{3}}$

$\dfrac{6}{3-\sqrt{3}} = \dfrac{6(3+\sqrt{3})}{(3-\sqrt{3})(3+\sqrt{3})} = \dfrac{6(3+\sqrt{3})}{9-3} = 3+\sqrt{3}$

    Answer $3+\sqrt{3}$ (2 marks)

9   Solve the simultaneous equations

$2x+y=15$

$x+y=8$

$2x+y=15$ (1)

$x+y=8$ (2)

Eq. (1)-Eq. (2) $\Rightarrow x=7 \Rightarrow y=8-7=1$ from Eq. (2)

    Answer $x=7, y=1$ (2 marks)

10 Solve $x^2+3x-10<0$

$x^2+3x-10<0 \Rightarrow (x-2)(x+5)<0 \Rightarrow -5<x<2$

    Answer $-5<x<2$ (2 marks)

12 Express 72 as the products of its prime factors.

Give your answer in index form.

$72 = 2\times2\times2\times3\times3 = 2^3\times3^2$

    Answer $2^3\times3^2$ (2 marks)

12 The scale of a map is such that 2 cm on the map represents an actual distance of 10 km.

12(a) Express the scale of the map as a ratio in the form 1: n where n is an integer.

2 cm : 10 km = 2 cm : 1000000 cm = 1:500000

Answer   1:500000   (2 marks)

12(b) The actual area of a park is 250 km². Calculate the area, in cm², of the park on the map.

$$\frac{250\,\text{km}^2}{500000^2} = \frac{250 \times (100000\,\text{cm})^2}{500000^2} = 10\,\text{cm}^2$$

Answer $10\,\text{cm}^2$ (2 marks)

13 20% of a number is 150.

Work out the number.

$$20\% \times x = 150 \Rightarrow x = \frac{150}{20\%} = 150 \times 5 = 750$$

Answer   750   (2 marks)

14 In a sale, all normal prices are reduced by 25%.

The normal price of a kettle is reduced by £3.00.

Work out the normal price of the kettle.

$$x \times 25\% = 3.00 \Rightarrow x = \frac{3.00}{25\%} = 12.00$$

Answer   £12.00   (2 marks)

15 Write 1.5×10^{-4} as an ordinary number.

Answer   0.00015   (2 marks)

16 Work out the value of $2.2 \times 10^5 \times (4 \times 10^3)$

Give your answer in standard form.

$2.2 \times 10^5 \times (4 \times 10^3) = 2.2 \times 4 \times 10^{5+3} = 8.8 \times 10^8$

Answer 8.8×10^8 (2 marks)

17   A large rectangle is made by joining four identical small rectangles as shown.

Diagram **NOT** accurately drawn

The perimeter of one small rectangle is 24 cm.

Work out the perimeter of the large rectangle.

The length of the small rectangle is 3 times its width.

width + length = 12 cm.

Width is $\frac{1}{4} \times 12\,\text{cm} = 3\,\text{cm}$

Length is $\frac{3}{4} \times 12\,\text{cm} = 9\,\text{cm}$

The perimeter of the large rectangle is $4 \times 9 + 2 \times 3 = 42$

Answer   42 cm   (3 marks)

18   Triangle *ABC* has perimeter 16cm

AB = 5 cm.

BC = 4 cm.

Show that *ABC* is an obtuse triangle.

$AC = 16 - 5 - 4 = 7$ which is the longest side in the triangle.

∴ $\angle B$ is the biggest angle in the triangle.

$\cos \angle B = \dfrac{AB^2 + BC^2 - AC^2}{2 \times AB \times BC} = \dfrac{25 + 16 - 49}{2 \times 5 \times 4} = -\dfrac{1}{5} < 0 \Rightarrow \angle B > 90°$

∴ *ABC* is an obtuse triangle.

(4 marks)

19 Here are a trapezium and a right-angled triangle. The area of the triangle is the same as the area of the trapezium.

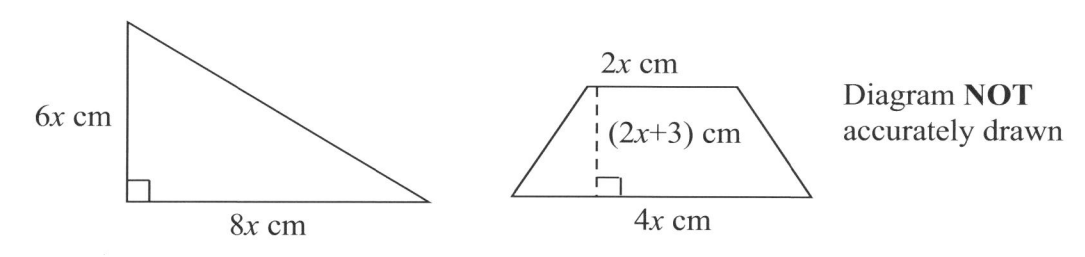

6x cm
8x cm
2x cm
(2x+3) cm
4x cm

Diagram **NOT** accurately drawn

Work out the value of x.

The area of the triangle is the same as the area of trapezium

$\frac{6x \times 8x}{2} = \frac{(2x+4x) \times (2x+3)}{2} \Rightarrow 6x(8x-2x-3) = 0 \Rightarrow x(6x-3) = 0 \Rightarrow x = 0 \text{ or } x = 0.5$

Clearly the solution, $x = 0$, is not suitable here.

Answer   0.5   (4 marks)

20 *AB* is a diameter of this circle and is extended to point *S*. *ST* is a tangent meeting the circle at point *T*. *O* is the centre of the circle. *AT = AO*

Prove that triangle *ATB* is congruent to triangle *OTS*.

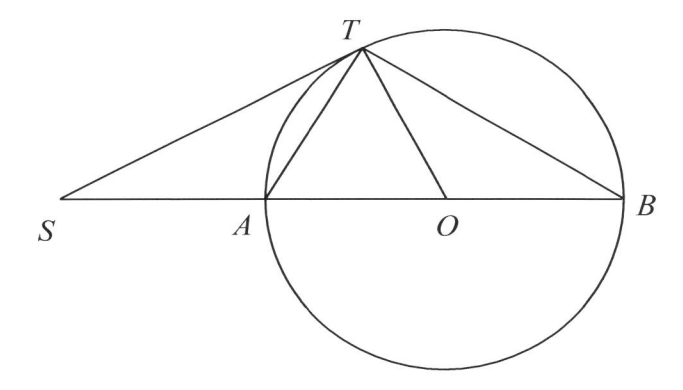

O is the centre of the circle, $\Rightarrow AO = OT$

$AT = AO \Rightarrow OT = AT = AO$, $\angle BAT = \angle SOT$

ST is a tangent meeting the circle at point $T \Rightarrow \angle OTS = 90°$

AB is a diameter of this circle $\Rightarrow \angle ATB = 90°$

$\Rightarrow \angle OTS = \angle ATB$

∴ Triangle *ATB* is congruent to triangle *OTS* (*ASA*)

(4 marks)

8

71

21 Here is the graph of $y = f(x)$

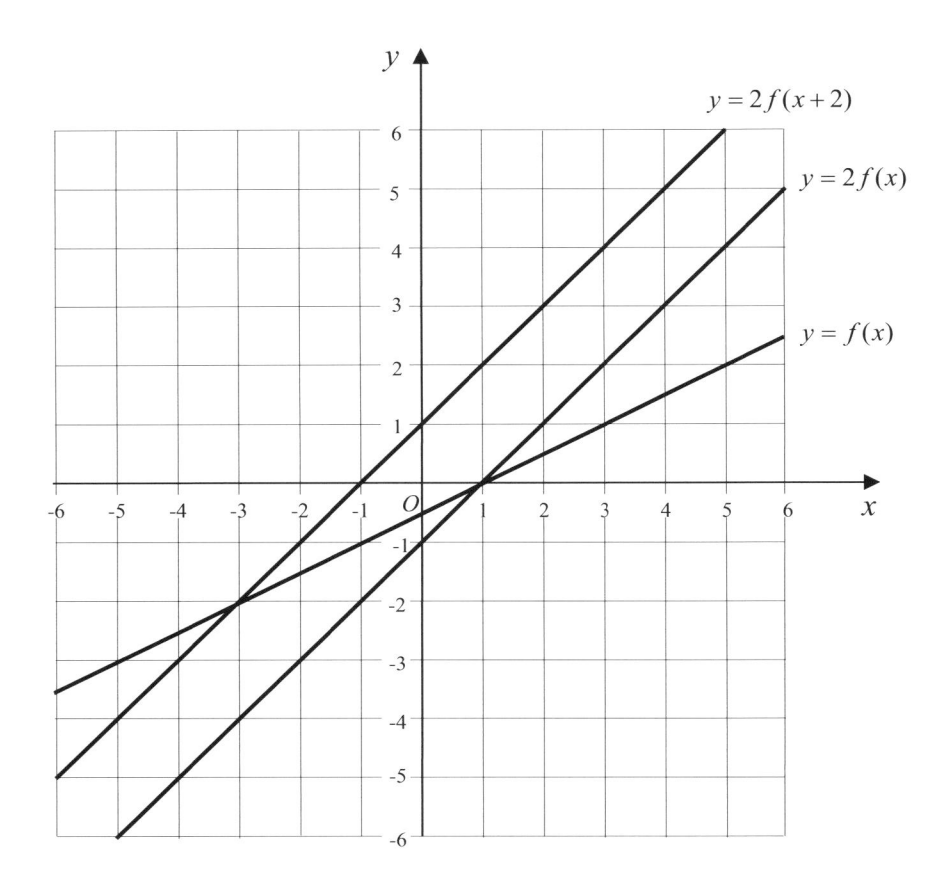

21(a) On the grid, draw the graph of $y = 2f(x)$

For the same x-coordinate on the graph of $y = f(x)$, the y-coordinate on the graph of $y = 2f(x)$ is twice the y-coordinate on the graph of $y = f(x)$. Therefore using two points on the graph $y = f(x)$, the coordinates on the graph of $y = 2f(x)$ can be calculated.

For example, points (1,0) and (3,1) are on the graph of $y = f(x)$, points (1,0) and (3,2) will be on the graph of $y = 2f(x)$. From points (1,0) and (3,2), the graph of $y = 2f(x)$ can be drawn.

(3 marks)

3

21(b) On the grid, draw the graph of $y = 2f(x+2)$

The graph of $y = 2f(x+2)$ can be drawn by translating the graph of $y = 2f(x)$, 2 squares to the left, as shown.

(3 marks)

22 The diagram shows a solid prism with the same cross-section through its length. The cross-section is a right-angled triangle with height 30 cm. The base *ABCD* is rectangle of width 20 cm and length 40 cm. The prism is made from wood with density 0.0005 kg/cm³.

Work out the mass of the prism.

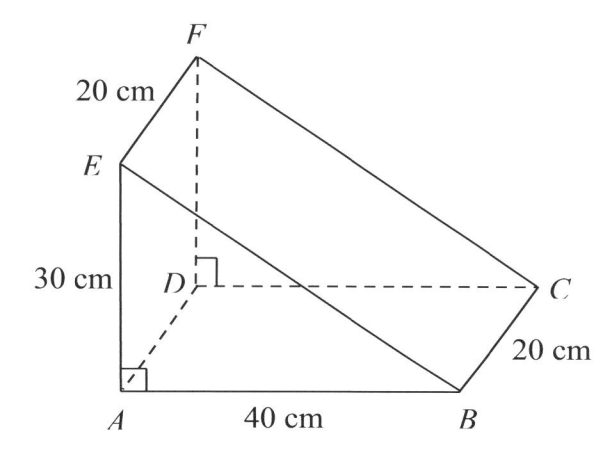

The prism has a height of 20 cm and the cross section with the right-angled triangle. The volume of the prism is:

$$\frac{AB \times AE}{2} \times BC$$

∴ The mass of the prism is

$$\frac{AB \times AE}{2} \times BC \times 0.0005 = \frac{40 \times 30}{2} \times 20 \times 0.0005 = 6$$

Answer   6 kg   (4 marks)

7

23   *OAB* is a triangle. *M* is the point on *AB* so that *AM:MB*=3:1

$\vec{OA} = \mathbf{x}$, $\vec{AB} = \mathbf{y}$.

Work out the vector of $\vec{OM}$

Give your answer in terms of **x** and **y**.

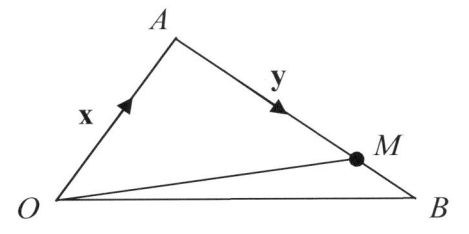

$AM{:}MB=3{:}1 \Rightarrow \vec{AM} = \dfrac{3\vec{AB}}{4} = \dfrac{3\mathbf{y}}{4}$

$\vec{OM} = \vec{OA} + \vec{AM} = \mathbf{x} + \dfrac{3\mathbf{y}}{4}$

Answer $\vec{OM} = \mathbf{x} + \dfrac{3\mathbf{y}}{4}$ (4 marks)

25   There are 7 blue marbles and 3 red marbles in a bag. Two marbles are taken at random from the bag.

24(a)   Calculate, as an exactly fraction, the probability that two marbles are different colour.

Two marbles are taken in this order, 1st blue, 2nd red. The probability is $\frac{7}{10} \times \frac{3}{9}$

Two marbles are taken in this order, 1st red, 2nd blue. The probability is $\frac{3}{10} \times \frac{7}{9}$

The probability that two marbles are different colour is $\frac{7}{10} \times \frac{3}{9} + \frac{3}{10} \times \frac{7}{9} = \frac{7}{15}$

Answer $\frac{7}{15}$ (3 marks)

24(b)   Calculate, as an exactly fraction, the probability that both marbles are the same colour.

The probability, when both are red marbles, is: $\frac{3}{10} \times \frac{2}{9}$

The probability, when both are blue marbles, is: $\frac{7}{10} \times \frac{6}{9}$

∴ The probability that both marbles are the same colour is: $\frac{3}{10} \times \frac{2}{9} + \frac{7}{10} \times \frac{6}{9} = \frac{8}{15}$

Answer $\frac{8}{15}$ (3 marks)

(Alternative method: by excluding the probability that two marbles are different colour, $1 - \frac{7}{15} = \frac{8}{15}$, where $\frac{7}{15}$ is from part (a) above)

25 The scatter graph shows the heights of boys at different ages.

25(a) Draw a line of best fit on the scatter graph.

(3 marks)

A line of best fit on the scatter graph is shown below

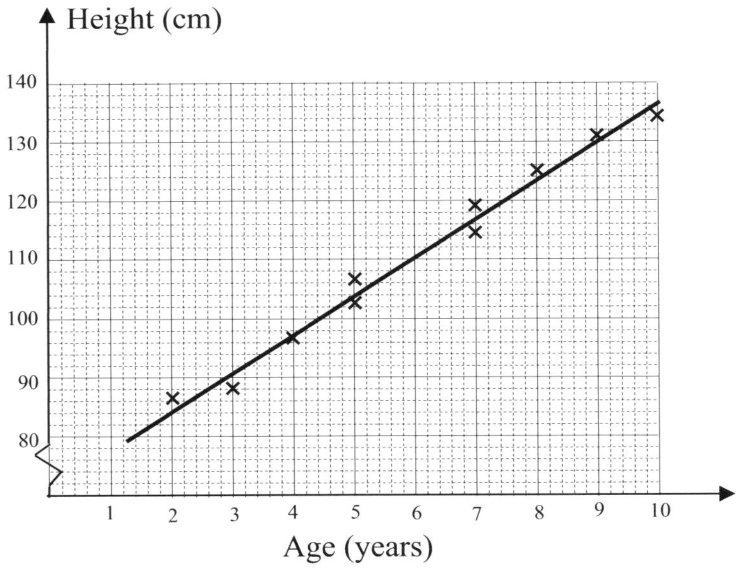

25(b) Estimate the height of a six year old.

Answer the height of a six year old is 110 cm

(3 marks)

6

Paper 3 solutions

1 One of these graphs is a sketch of $y = -\dfrac{x^2 + x - 2}{2}$

   Which one?

   Circle the correct letter.

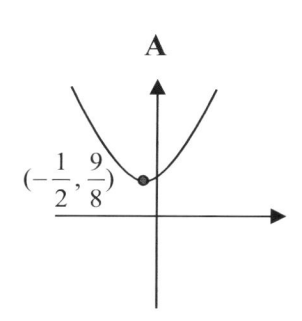

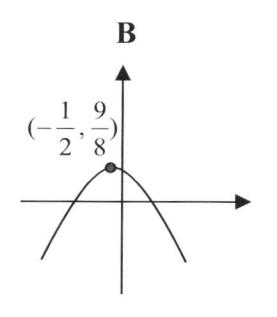

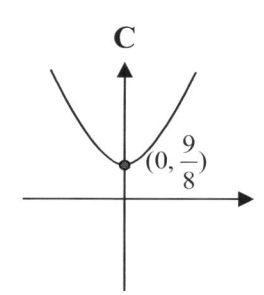

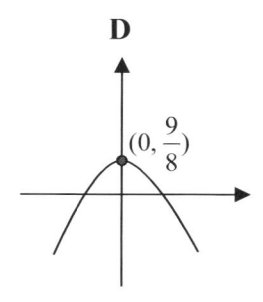

   A (parabola opening up, vertex $(-\tfrac{1}{2}, \tfrac{9}{8})$)

   B (parabola opening down, vertex $(-\tfrac{1}{2}, \tfrac{9}{8})$)

   C (parabola opening up, vertex $(0, \tfrac{9}{8})$)

   D (parabola opening down, vertex $(0, \tfrac{9}{8})$)

   Answer **B** (2 marks)

2 What is 950 million in standard form?

   Circle your answer.

   950×10^6 95×10^7 9.5×10^8 0.95×10^9 9.5×10^9 9.5×10^{10}

   Answer 9.5×10^8 (2 marks)

3 Average speed = $\dfrac{\text{distance}}{\text{time}}$

   If the distance is doubled and the time is halved, what happens to the average speed?

   Circle your answer.

   ×2   ×4   no change   ÷2   ÷4

   Answer ×4 (2 marks)

6

77

4   The first four terms of a geometric progression are

    2   8   32   128

    Work out an expression, in terms of *n*, for the *n*th term.

    $a_n = a_1 r^{n-1}$

    $\Rightarrow a_2 = a_1 r \Rightarrow r = \dfrac{a_2}{a_1} = \dfrac{8}{2} = 4$, where $n = 2$.

    $\therefore a_n = 2 \times 4^{n-1}$

       Answer $a_n = 2 \times 4^{n-1}$ (3 marks)

5   Triangle **A** and triangle **B** are similar.

    Triangle **A** has a circumference of 150 cm

    Triangle **B** has a circumference of 30 cm

    Triangle **B** has an area of 40 cm^2

    Circle your answer for the area of triangle **A**.

    200 cm^2 400 cm^2 1000 cm^2 2000 cm^2

    The area of triangle **A** can be calculated as follows:

    $\dfrac{\text{Circumference }\mathbf{A}}{\text{Circumference }\mathbf{B}} = \sqrt{\dfrac{\text{Area }\mathbf{A}}{\text{Area }\mathbf{B}}} \Rightarrow \text{Area }\mathbf{A} = \left(\dfrac{\text{Circumference }\mathbf{A}}{\text{Circumference }\mathbf{B}}\right)^2 \times \text{Area }\mathbf{B}$

    $\text{Area }\mathbf{A} = \left(\dfrac{150}{30}\right)^2 \times 40 = 1000$

       Answer   1000 cm^2 (3 marks)

6   Circle the calculation that decreases 400 by 7%

    400×0.07 400×0.93 400×0.3 400×0.7

    $400 \times (1 - 7\%) = 400 \times (1 - 0.07) = 400 \times 0.93$

       Answer 400×0.93 (2 marks)

7 Calculate $27^{-\frac{1}{3}}$.

Circle your answer.

$\quad 3 \qquad \frac{1}{3} \qquad -3 \qquad -\frac{1}{3}$

$27^{-\frac{1}{3}} = \frac{1}{27^{\frac{1}{3}}} = \frac{1}{3}$

Answer $\quad \frac{1}{3} \quad$ (2 marks)

8 Simplify $\dfrac{\sqrt{2^5}}{(\sqrt{2})^3}$

$\dfrac{\sqrt{2^5}}{(\sqrt{2})^3} = \dfrac{2^{\frac{5}{2}}}{2^{\frac{3}{2}}} = 2^{\frac{5}{2}-\frac{3}{2}} = 2$

Answer $\quad 2 \quad$ (2 marks)

(Alternative method: $\dfrac{\sqrt{2^5}}{(\sqrt{2})^3} = \dfrac{(\sqrt{2})^5}{(\sqrt{2})^3} = (\sqrt{2})^{5-3} = 2$)

9 Circle the expression that is equivalent to $(2a^3b^4)^3$

$\quad 8a^9b^{12} \qquad 8a^3b^7 \qquad 8a^6b^7 \qquad 6a^6b^7$

$(2a^3b^4)^3 = 2^3 a^{3\times 3} b^{4\times 3} = 8a^9b^{12}$

Answer $\quad 8a^9b^{12} \quad$ (2 marks)

10 Solve $x^3 = x(2x+3)$

$x^3 = x(2x+3) \Rightarrow x(x^2 - 2x - 3) = 0 \Rightarrow x(x-3)(x+1) \Rightarrow x = 0, 3 \text{ or } -1$

Answer $\quad -1, 0, 3 \quad$ (3 marks)

11 Solve $\sqrt{12} + \sqrt{48} = \sqrt{27} + \sqrt{x}$

$\sqrt{12} + \sqrt{48} = \sqrt{27} + \sqrt{x} \Rightarrow 2\sqrt{3} + 4\sqrt{3} = 3\sqrt{3} + \sqrt{x} \Rightarrow \sqrt{x} = 3\sqrt{3} \Rightarrow x = 27$

Answer $\quad 27 \quad$ (3 marks)

12   Here are three numbers written in standard form.

Arrange these numbers in order of size.

Start with the smallest number.

3.5×10^{-7} 7.5×10^{-8} 2.5×10^{-6}

Answer 7.5×10^{-8} 3.5×10^{-7} 2.5×10^{-6}

(2 marks)

13   Factorise fully $(x^2 - 16) - (x+4)^2 + (x+4)(x+1)$

$(x^2 - 16) - (x+4)^2 + (x+4)(x+1)$
$= (x+4)(x-4) - (x+4)^2 + (x+4)(x+1)$
$= (x+4)(x-4-x-4+x+1)$
$= (x+4)(x-7)$

Answer $(x+4)(x-7)$ (3 marks)

14   Expand and simplify $(3x+4y)(4x-3y)$

$(3x+4y)(4x-3y) = 12x^2 + 16xy - 9xy - 12y^2 = 12x^2 + 7xy - 12y^2$

Answer $12x^2 + 7xy - 12y^2$ (3 marks)

15   Write as a single fraction $\dfrac{6}{x^2 - 9} + \dfrac{1}{x+3}$

Give your answer in its simplest form.

$\dfrac{6}{x^2 - 9} + \dfrac{1}{x+3} = \dfrac{6}{(x-3)(x+3)} + \dfrac{1}{x+3} = \dfrac{6 + x - 3}{(x-3)(x+3)} = \dfrac{1}{x-3}$

Answer $\dfrac{1}{x-3}$ (3 marks)

16   Simplify $\dfrac{\cos 45° + \sin 30°}{\tan 60°}$

Give your answer in the form $\dfrac{\sqrt{a} + \sqrt{b}}{c}$, where a, b and c are integers.

$\dfrac{\cos 45° + \sin 30°}{\tan 60°} = \dfrac{\frac{\sqrt{2}}{2} + \frac{1}{2}}{\sqrt{3}} = \dfrac{\sqrt{2} \times \sqrt{3} + \sqrt{3}}{2\sqrt{3} \times \sqrt{3}} = \dfrac{\sqrt{6} + \sqrt{3}}{6}$

Answer $\dfrac{\sqrt{6} + \sqrt{3}}{6}$ (3 marks)

17 $0.0\dot{3} = \dfrac{1}{30}$

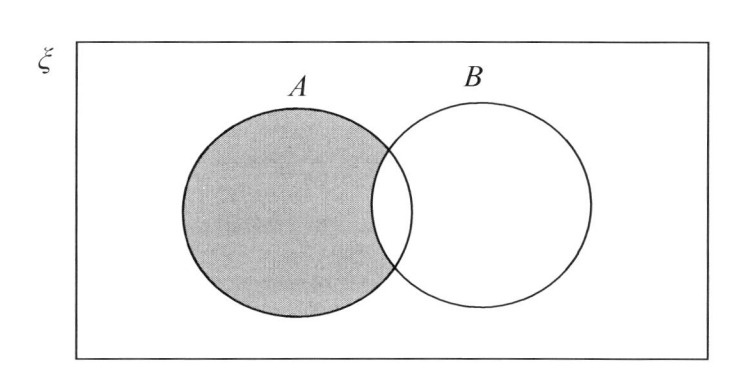

Use this fact to show that $0.1\dot{3} = \dfrac{2}{15}$

$0.1\dot{3} = 0.1 + 0.0\dot{3} = \dfrac{1}{10} + \dfrac{1}{30} = \dfrac{3}{30} + \dfrac{1}{30} = \dfrac{4}{30} = \dfrac{2}{15}$

$\therefore 0.1\dot{3} = \dfrac{2}{15}$

(3 marks)

18 y is inversely proportional to x.

Complete the table.

$y = \dfrac{k}{x} \Rightarrow k = xy \Rightarrow k = 2 \times 6 = 12$

$y = \dfrac{12}{x} \Rightarrow y_1 = \dfrac{12}{3} = 4$

$x = \dfrac{k}{y} \Rightarrow x_2 = \dfrac{12}{24} = \dfrac{1}{2}$

x	3	2	$\dfrac{1}{2}$
y	4	6	24

(3 marks)

19 Which of these represents the shaded region?

Circle your answer.

$A \cup B'$ A' $A \cap B'$ B'

Answer $A \cap B'$ (2 marks)

8

20 Here is a triangle.

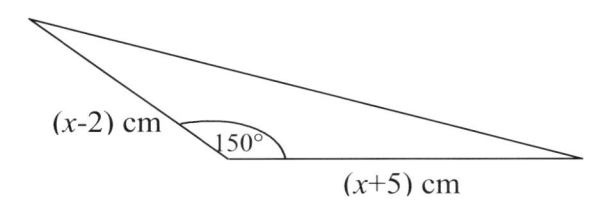

(x-2) cm, 150°, (x+5) cm

20(a) Show the area of the triangle is $\dfrac{x^2+3x-10}{4}$ cm²

The area of the triangle can be calculated as follows:

$$\dfrac{(x+5)\times(x-2)}{2}\times\sin 150° = \dfrac{x^2+3x-10}{2}\times\dfrac{1}{2} = \dfrac{x^2+3x-10}{4}$$

∴ The area of the triangle is $\dfrac{x^2+3x-10}{4}$ cm²

(4 marks)

20(b) The area of the triangle is greater than 11 cm².

Work out the range of the possible values of x

Give your answer as an inequality.

$\dfrac{x^2+3x-10}{4} > 11 \Rightarrow x^2+3x-54 > 0 \Rightarrow (x-6)(x+9) > 0 \Rightarrow x > 6$ or $x < -9$

If $x < -9$, $x-2 < -11$, it clearly shows that the solution for $x < -9$ is not suitable here.

∴ $x > 6$

Answer $x > 6$ (3 marks)

21 There are

8 different sandwiches

5 different drinks

and

3 different snacks.

Meal Deal
Choose one sandwich, one drink and one snack

21(a) How many different Meal Deal combinations are there?

$8 \times 5 \times 3 = 120$

Answer   120   (4 marks)

21 (b) Two of the sandwiches have cheese in them.

Three of the drinks are fizzy.

Emma picks a Meal Deal at random.

Work out the probability that the sandwich has cheese in it and the drink is fizzy.

Give your answer as a fraction in its simplest form.

Meal Deal combinations for the cheese sandwich and fizzy drink are:

$2 \times 3 \times 3 = 18$

The probability, that the sandwich has cheese in it and the drink is fizzy, is:

$\dfrac{18}{120} = \dfrac{3}{20}$

Answer $\dfrac{3}{20}$ (4 marks)

(Alternative method: the probability, that the sandwich has cheese in it, is $\dfrac{2}{8}$;

the probability, that the drink is fizzy, is $\dfrac{3}{5}$; the probability, that the sandwich has

cheese in it and the drink is fizzy, is: $\dfrac{2}{8} \times \dfrac{3}{5} = \dfrac{3}{20}$)

4

22 The sketch shows part of a circle, and a line $y = -2x + 6$. The line passes the centre of the circle. The circle intersects the y-axis at points A and B.

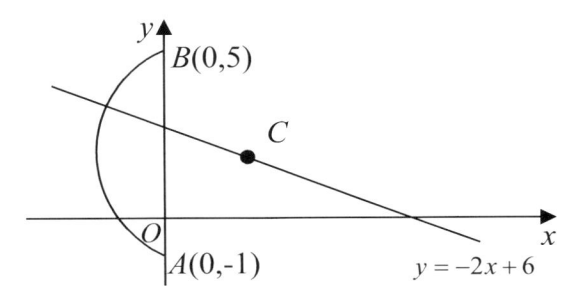

Work out the equation of the circle.

$C(C_x, C_y)$ is the centre of the circle. The circle intersects the y-axis at points A and B. $C_y = \dfrac{A_y + B_y}{2} = \dfrac{5-1}{2} = 2$

The line passes the centre of the circle, $\therefore C_y = -2C_x + 6 \Rightarrow C_x = \dfrac{6 - C_y}{2} = \dfrac{6-2}{2} = 2$

The radius of the circle is $AC = \sqrt{(C_y - A_y)^2 + (C_x - A_x)^2} = \sqrt{(2+1)^2 + (2-0)^2} = \sqrt{13}$

The equation of the circle is $(x-2)^2 + (y-2)^2 = 13$

Answer $(x-2)^2 + (y-2)^2 = 13$ (5 marks)

23 The diagram shows the graph of $y = \cos x$ for $0° \leq x \leq 360°$

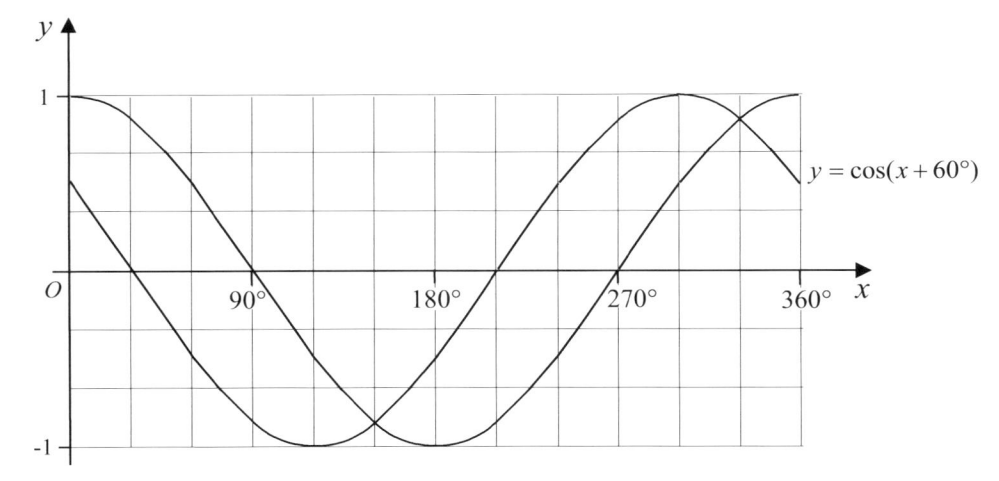

On the grid above, sketch the graph of $y = \cos(x + 60°)$ for $0° \leq x \leq 360°$

The graph of $y = \cos(x + 60°)$ can be drawn by translating the graph of $y = \cos x$, 60° to the left, as shown on the graph.   (4 marks)

24. The table gives information about the areas of some farms in France.

Area (*A* hectares)	Frequency
$0 < A \leq 20$	50
$20 < A \leq 50$	90
$50 < A \leq 100$	120
$100 < A \leq 300$	180

On the grid, draw a histogram to show this information.

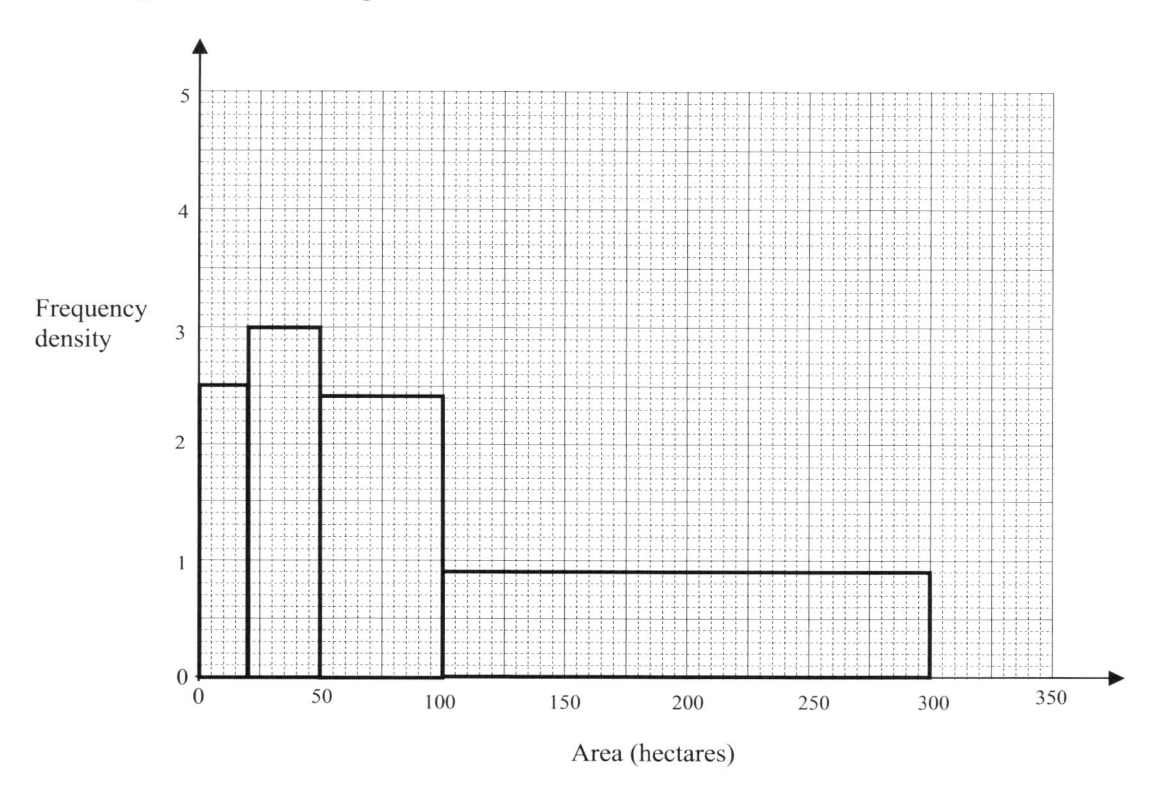

$0 < A \leq 20$, Frequency density: $\frac{50}{20} = 2.5$

$20 < A \leq 50$, Frequency density: $\frac{90}{30} = 3$

$50 < A \leq 100$, Frequency density: $\frac{120}{50} = 2.4$

$100 < A \leq 300$, Frequency density: $\frac{180}{200} = 0.9$

The histogram is drawn, as shown.

(4 marks)

25 The table shows information about the number of fish caught by 29 people in a club in one day.

Jack is one of the 29 people in the club.

Number of fish	Frequency
0	2
1	6
2	10
3	8
5	2
8	1

The number of fish caught by him was the same as the median number of fish caught for his club.

Work out the number of fish caught by him.

$\frac{29+1}{2} = 15$, Jack is in the 15th position for the number of fish caught for his club, so that the number of fish caught by him is 2.

Answer   2   (4 marks)

Paper 4 solutions

1 Circle the number that is closest in value to $\dfrac{9.999}{0.0499}$

    2   20   200   2000

$\dfrac{9.999}{0.0499} \approx \dfrac{10}{0.05} = \dfrac{1000}{5} = 200$

    Answer   200   (2 marks)

2 Below are three sequences:

    A: Quadratic sequence;   B: Arithmetic sequence;

    C: Geometric progression

    Which sequence does each of the three below belong to? Circle your answer.

2(a)   2   6   10   14   …   A   B   C

2(b)   2   8   32   128   …   A   B   C

2(c)   101   104   109   116   …   A   B   C

2(a)   2   6   10   14   …   A   B   C

    The *n*th term of the sequence is $2 + 4(n-1)$

        Answer   B   (1 marks)

2(b)   2   8   32   128   …   A   B   C

    The *n*th term of the sequence is $2 \times 4^{n-1}$

        Answer   C   (1 marks)

2(c)   101   104   109   116   …   A   B   C

    The *n*th term of the sequence is $100 + n^2$

        Answer   A   (1 marks)

3   Solid **A** and Solid **B** are mathematically similar.

Solid **A** has a volume of 8000 cm^3

Solid **B** has a volume of 1000 cm^3

Solid **A** has surface area 4000 cm^2

Circle your answer for the surface area of solid **B**.

1000 cm^2 2000 cm^2 4000 cm^2 8000 cm^2

The surface area of solid **B** can be calculated as follows:

$$\sqrt[3]{\frac{\text{Volume B}}{\text{Volume A}}} = \sqrt{\frac{\text{Area B}}{\text{Area A}}} \Rightarrow \text{Area B} = \left(\sqrt[3]{\frac{\text{Volume B}}{\text{Volume A}}}\right)^2 \times \text{Area A}$$

$$\left(\sqrt[3]{\frac{1000}{8000}}\right)^2 \times 4000 = 1000$$

Answer   1000 cm^2 (2 marks)

4   Volume = $\frac{\text{mass}}{\text{density}}$

The mass of solid A is 9 times the mass of solid B.

The density of solid A is 3 times the density of solid B.

Complete the sentence.

The volume of solid A is …………………………..times the volume of solid B.

Answer   3   (2 marks)

5   *P* is directly proportional to Q^2 where $Q > 0$. $P = 400$ when $Q = 4$.

5(a)   Find a formula for *P* in terms of *Q*.

$P = kQ^2$ where *k* is a constant.

$k = \frac{P}{Q^2} = \frac{400}{4^2} = 25$

$\therefore P = 25Q^2$

Answer $P = 25Q^2$ (2 marks)

6

5(b) Find the value of Q when $P=100$.

$P = 25Q^2 \Rightarrow Q = \pm\sqrt{\dfrac{P}{25}}$

$\because Q > 0$, clearly the negative answer is not suitable here.

$Q = \sqrt{\dfrac{P}{25}} = \sqrt{\dfrac{100}{25}} = 2$

Answer   2   (2 marks)

6(a) Work out $2\dfrac{1}{6} + 1\dfrac{3}{4}$

$2\dfrac{1}{6} + 1\dfrac{3}{4} = 2\dfrac{2}{12} + 1\dfrac{9}{12} = 3\dfrac{11}{12}$

Answer $3\dfrac{11}{12}$ (2 marks)

6(b) Work out $1\dfrac{3}{5} \div \dfrac{4}{7}$

Give your answer as a mixed number in its simplest form.

$1\dfrac{3}{5} \div \dfrac{4}{7} = \dfrac{\cancel{8}^{2}}{5} \times \dfrac{7}{\cancel{4}_{1}} = \dfrac{14}{5} = 2\dfrac{4}{5}$

Answer $2\dfrac{4}{5}$ (2 marks)

7   60% of p = 20% of q.

Work out an expression of p, as a fraction in its simplest form, in terms of q.

$60\%\, p = 20\%\, q \Rightarrow p = \dfrac{20}{60}q \Rightarrow p = \dfrac{1}{3}q$

Answer $p = \dfrac{1}{3}q$ (2 marks)

8   Factorise fully $4x^4 - 16x^2$.

$4x^4 - 16x^2 = 4x^2(x^2 - 4) = 4x^2(x-2)(x+2)$

Answer $4x^2(x-2)(x+2)$ (2 marks)

10

9   $x:y = 3:2$ and $y:z = 5:8$

Work out $x:y:z$

Give your answer in its simplest form.

$x:y = 3:2 = 15:10$, $y:z = 5:8 = 10:16$

$\therefore x:y:z = 15:10:16$

Answer $15:10:16$ (2 marks)

10 Solve $4^{\frac{1}{8}} \times 2^x = 8^{\frac{3}{4}}$

$4^{\frac{1}{8}} \times 2^x = 8^{\frac{3}{4}} \Rightarrow (2^2)^{\frac{1}{8}} \times 2^x = (2^3)^{\frac{3}{4}} \Rightarrow 2^{\frac{1}{4}+x} = 2^{\frac{9}{4}} \Rightarrow \frac{1}{4} + x = \frac{9}{4} \Rightarrow x = 2$

Answer   2   (2 marks)

11 Solve $\dfrac{2}{2x+1} + \dfrac{1}{4x^2-1} = 1$

$\dfrac{2}{2x+1} + \dfrac{1}{4x^2-1} = 1 \Rightarrow \dfrac{2(2x-1)}{(2x+1)(2x-1)} + \dfrac{1}{(2x+1)(2x-1)} - \dfrac{4x^2-1}{(2x+1)(2x-1)} = 0 \Rightarrow$

$\dfrac{-4x^2+4x}{(2x+1)(2x-1)} = 0 \Rightarrow \dfrac{4x(-x+1)}{(2x+1)(2x-1)} = 0 \Rightarrow x=0$ or $x=1$

Answer   0, 1   (2 marks)

12 Write 2.3×10^{-4} as an ordinary number.

Circle your answer.

0.00023   0.0023   0.023   0.023

Answer   0.00023   (1 mark)

13 Simplify $\sqrt{128} - \sqrt{98}$

$\sqrt{128} - \sqrt{98} = 8\sqrt{2} - 7\sqrt{2} = \sqrt{2}$

Answer $\sqrt{2}$ (2 marks)

14 Write $(2\sqrt{3} + 3\sqrt{2})^2$ in the form $p + q\sqrt{6}$, where p and q are integers.

$(2\sqrt{3} + 3\sqrt{2})^2 = (2\sqrt{3})^2 + (3\sqrt{2})^2 + 2 \times 2\sqrt{3} \times 3\sqrt{2} = 30 + 12\sqrt{6}$

Answer $30 + 12\sqrt{6}$ (2 marks)

15 Using algebra, prove that $\dfrac{0.\dot{3}\dot{6}}{0.\dot{3}}$ is equal in value to $1\dfrac{1}{11}$

$x = 0.\dot{3}\dot{6}$ (1)

$100x = 36.\dot{3}\dot{6}$ (2)

Eq. (2)-Eq. (1) $\Rightarrow 99x = 36 \Rightarrow x = \dfrac{36}{99} = \dfrac{4}{11}$

$y = 0.\dot{3}$ (3)

$10y = 3.\dot{3}$ (4)

Eq. (4)-Eq. (3) $\Rightarrow 9y = 3 \Rightarrow y = \dfrac{3}{9} = \dfrac{1}{3}$

$\dfrac{0.\dot{3}\dot{6}}{0.\dot{3}} = \dfrac{\frac{4}{11}}{\frac{1}{3}} = \dfrac{4}{11} \times 3 = \dfrac{12}{11} = 1\dfrac{1}{11}$

$\therefore \dfrac{0.\dot{3}\dot{6}}{0.\dot{3}} = 1\dfrac{1}{11}$

(3 marks)

16 Prove that $\dfrac{\tan 60° + \tan 45°}{\sin 60° + \sin 30°}$ is an integer.

$\dfrac{\tan 60° + \tan 45°}{\sin 60° + \sin 30°} = \dfrac{\sqrt{3}+1}{\frac{\sqrt{3}}{2}+\frac{1}{2}} = \dfrac{2(\sqrt{3}+1)}{\sqrt{3}+1} = 2$

$\therefore \dfrac{\tan 60° + \tan 45°}{\sin 60° + \sin 30°}$ is an integer.

(3 marks)

17 x kg = y lbs

Write a formula for y in terms of x, by using 5 kg=11 lbs.

x kg = y lbs   (1)

5 kg=11 lbs   (2)

Eq. (1) $\div$ Eq. (2) $\Rightarrow \dfrac{x}{5} = \dfrac{y}{11} \Rightarrow y = \dfrac{11}{5}x$

Answer $y = \dfrac{11}{5}x$ (3 marks)

18   Here is a triangle.

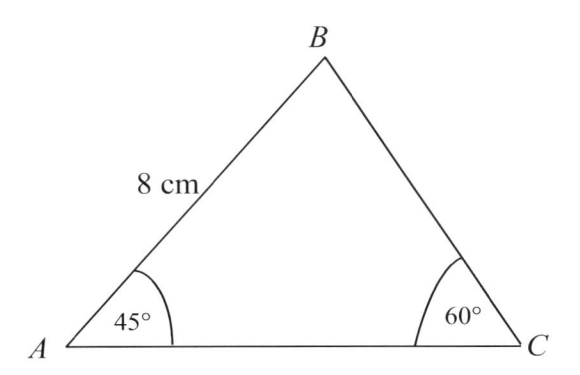

   Work out the length of BC.

   $$\frac{8}{\sin 60°} = \frac{BC}{\sin 45°} \Rightarrow BC = \frac{8}{\sin 60°} \sin 45° \Rightarrow BC = \frac{8}{\frac{\sqrt{3}}{2}} \times \frac{\sqrt{2}}{2} = \frac{8}{3}\sqrt{6}$$

   Answer $\frac{8}{3}\sqrt{6}$ cm   (3 marks)

19   ABC is an isosceles triangle. AC is a tangent to the circle.

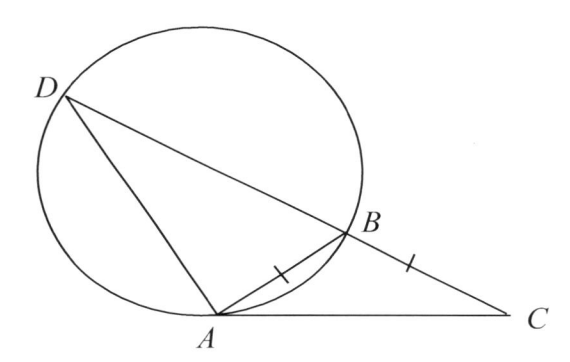

   Prove that ACD is an isosceles triangle.

   ABC is an isosceles triangle, ∴ ∠CAB = ∠C   (1)

   AC is a tangent to the circle, ∴ ∠CAB = ∠D   (2)

   ∴ ∠C = ∠D, from Eqs. (1) and (2)

   ∴ ACD is an isosceles triangle.

                                (3 marks)

20   The distance-time graph shows information about part of a car journey.

20(a)   Work out the average speed during the 6 seconds.

$$\frac{180}{6} = 30$$

Answer   30 m/s   (3 marks)

20(b)   Use the graph to estimate the speed of the car at time 2 seconds.

Give your answer to 1 decimal place.

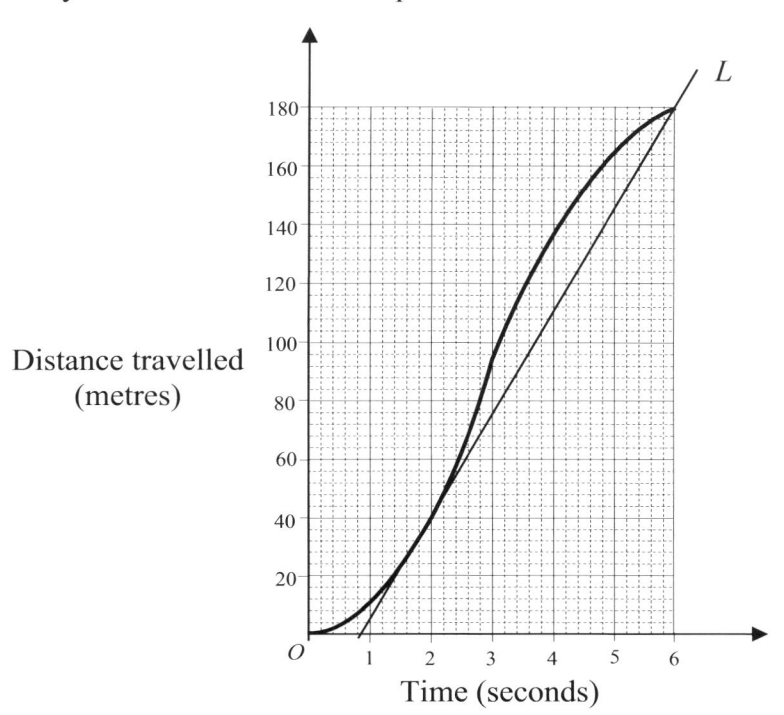

Draw a tangent at time 2 seconds, labelled *L* on the graph. It passes through (2,40) and (6, 180).

The gradient of *L* is: $\frac{180-40}{6-2} = \frac{140}{4} = 35$

Answer   35 m/s   (3 marks)

21 A line passes through $(3,4)$ and $(6,10)$.

Work out the equation of the line.

Give your answer in the form $y = mx + c$

$y - 4 = \dfrac{10-4}{6-3} \times (x-3) \Rightarrow y - 4 = 2(x-3) \Rightarrow y = 2x - 2$

Answer $\quad y = 2x - 2$ (2 marks)

22 The graph shows two lines A and B.

The equation of line B is $y = \dfrac{1}{2}x + \dfrac{7}{2}$. The two lines are perpendicular each other and intersect at $(1,4)$

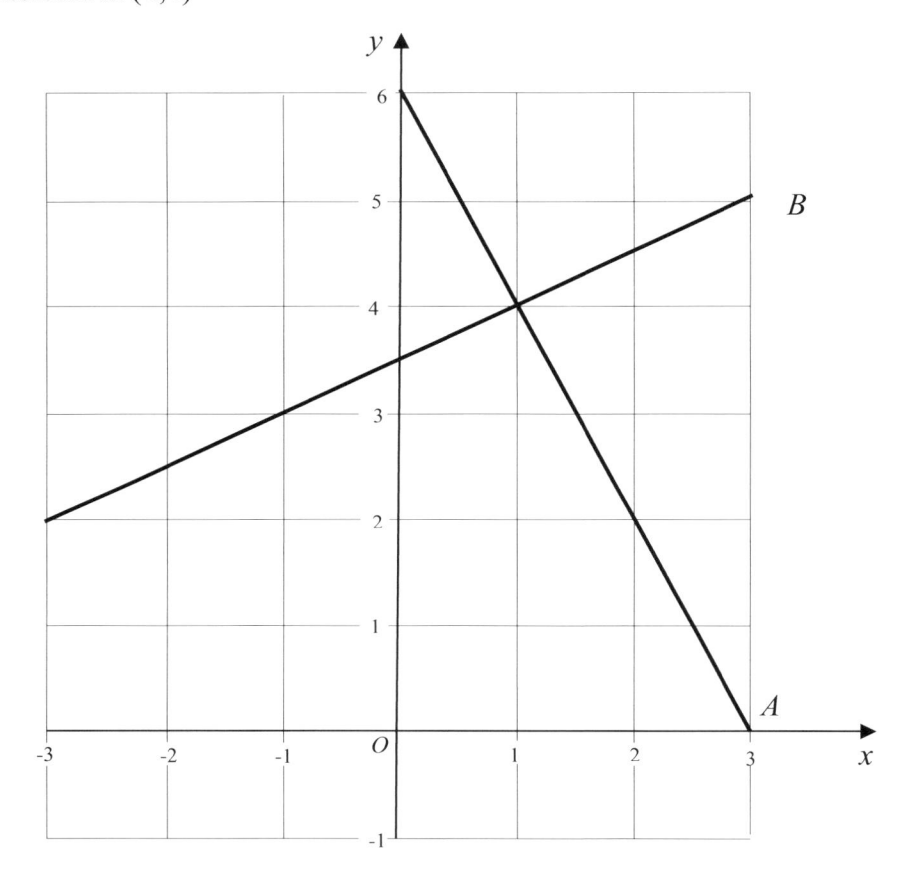

Work out the equation of line A.

Lines A and B intersect at $(1,4)$, and the two lines are perpendicular each other.

∴ The equation of line A is:

$y - 4 = -2(x-1) \Rightarrow y = -2x + 6$

Answer $\quad y = -2x + 6$ (3 marks)

23(a) On the diagram, draw the image of Shape A when it is reflected in the *x*-axis.

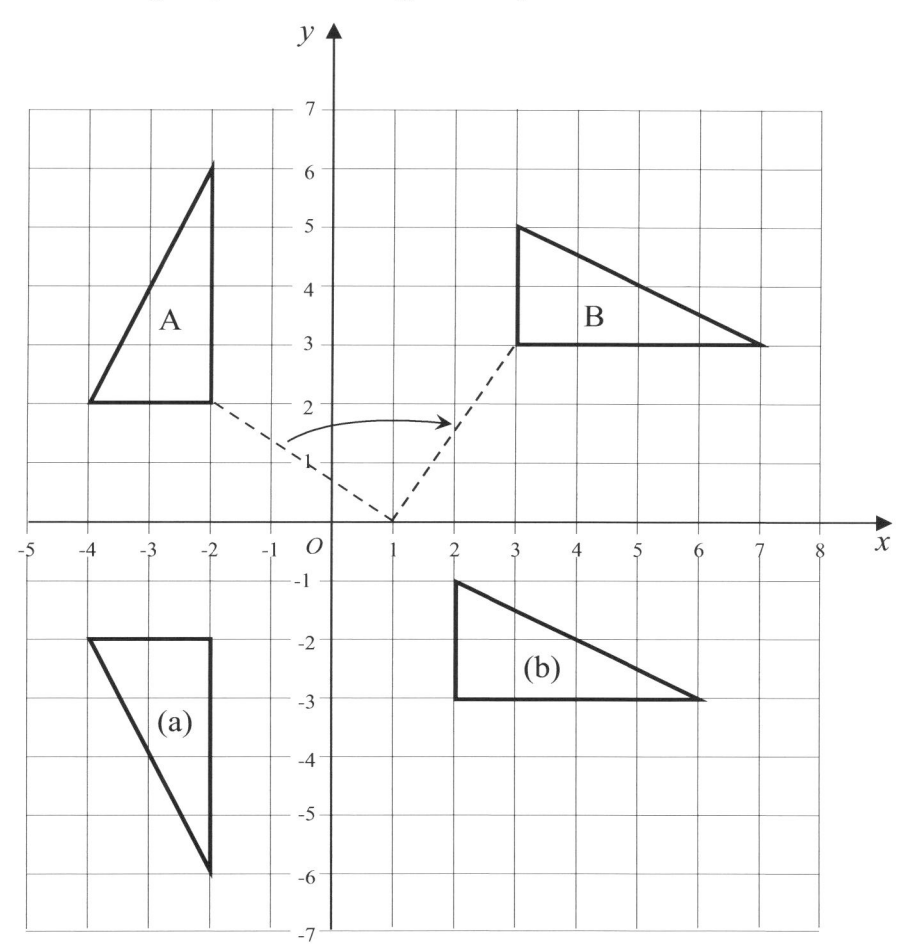

As shown on the diagram.

(3 marks)

23(b) On the diagram, draw the image of Shape B when it is translated by the vector $\begin{pmatrix} -1 \\ -6 \end{pmatrix}$

As shown on the diagram.

(3 marks)

23(c) Describe fully the single transformation which will map Shape A onto Shape B.
Rotation 90° clockwise about (1,0).

(3 marks)

24 There are 9 counters in a bag.

There is a number on each counter.

① ① ② ② ② ③ ③ ③ ③

Jack takes at random 2 counters from the bag.

He adds together the numbers on the 2 counters to get his Total.

24(a) Complete and fully label the probability tree diagram to show the possible outcome.

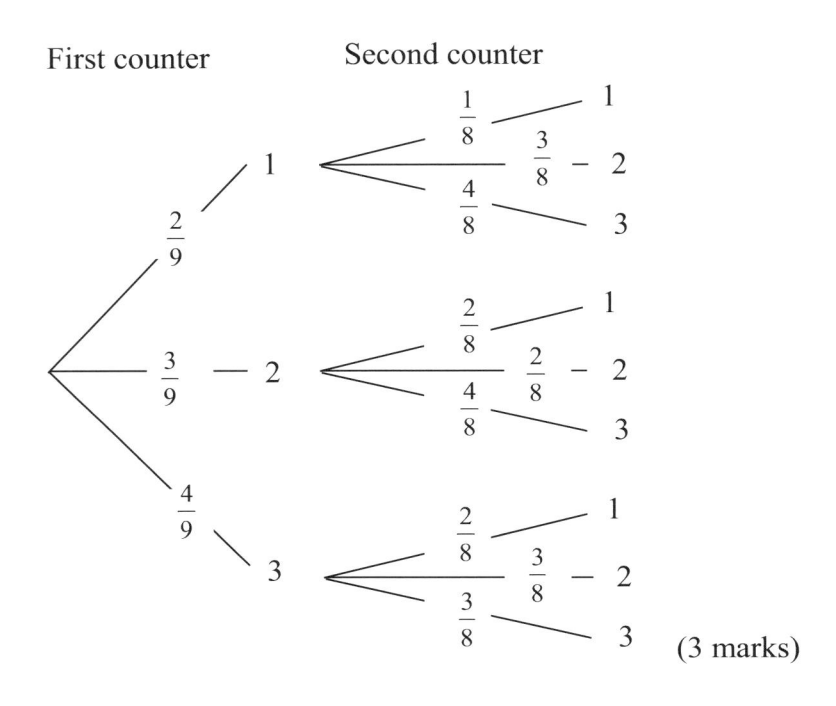

First counter   Second counter

$\frac{2}{9}$ — 1 $\begin{cases} \frac{1}{8} - 1 \\ \frac{3}{8} - 2 \\ \frac{4}{8} - 3 \end{cases}$

$\frac{3}{9}$ — 2 $\begin{cases} \frac{2}{8} - 1 \\ \frac{2}{8} - 2 \\ \frac{4}{8} - 3 \end{cases}$

$\frac{4}{9}$ — 3 $\begin{cases} \frac{2}{8} - 1 \\ \frac{3}{8} - 2 \\ \frac{3}{8} - 3 \end{cases}$

(3 marks)

24(b) Work out the probability that his Total is greater than 3.

Give your answer as a fraction in its simplest form.

From the probability tree diagram, the probability, that his Total is greater than 3, can be calculated as follows.

$\frac{2}{9} \times \frac{4}{8} + \frac{3}{9} \times (\frac{2}{8} + \frac{4}{8}) + \frac{4}{9} = \frac{29}{36}$

Answer $\frac{29}{36}$ (2 marks)

5

96

25 The cumulative frequency table shows information about the height of 50 men.

Height (h cm)	Cumulative frequency
$150 < h \leq 160$	5
$150 < h \leq 170$	15
$150 < h \leq 180$	35
$150 < h \leq 190$	45
$150 < h \leq 200$	50

25(a) On the grid, draw a cumulative frequency graph for the table.

As shown on the diagram.

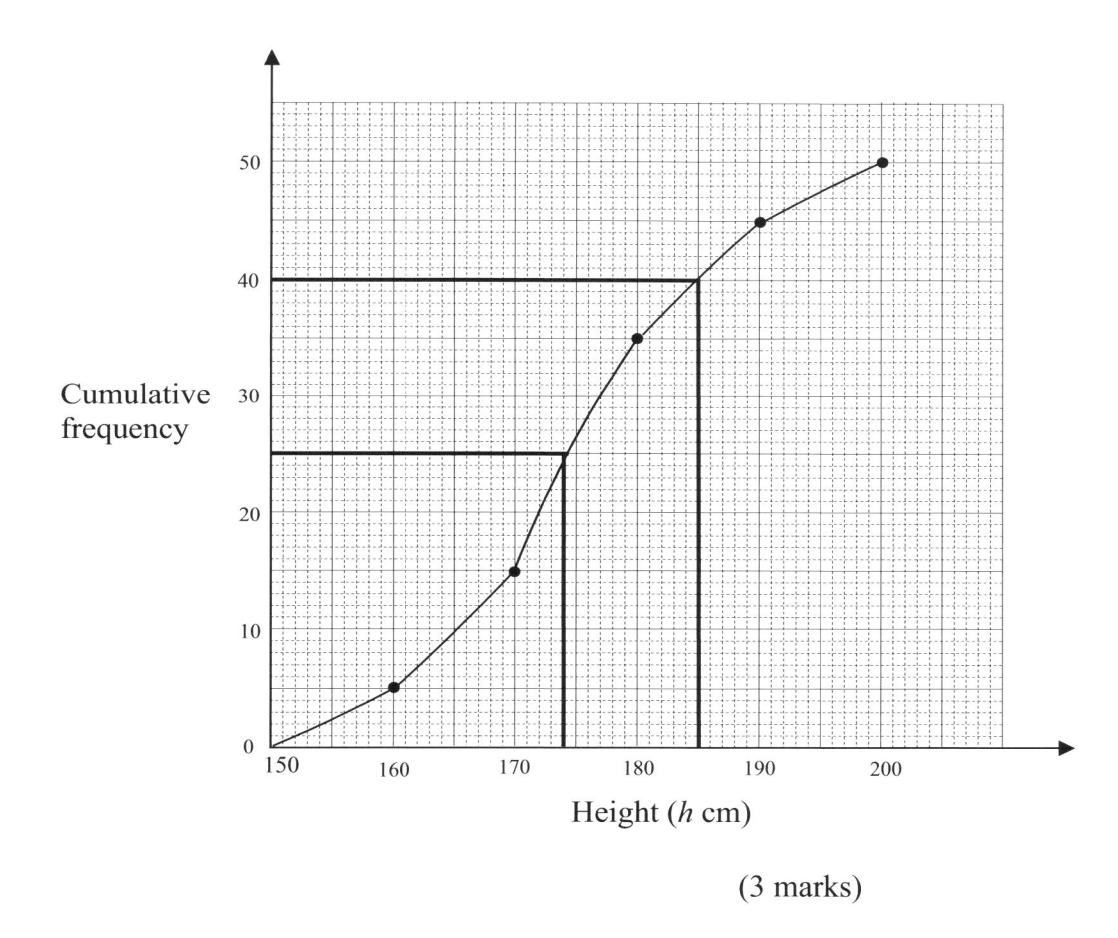

(3 marks)

25(b) Use your graph to find an estimate for the median height of the 50 men.

174 cm, as shown on the diagram.

Answer   174 cm   (3 marks)

25(c) Use your graph to find an estimate for the number of the men who are taller than 185 cm.

From the cumulative frequency graph, the number of the men who are 185 cm and shorter than 185 cm is 40.

The number of the men, who are taller than 185 cm, is:

$50 - 40 = 10$

Answer   10   (2 marks)

Printed in Great Britain
by Amazon